Janet Sternburg is an essayist and poet, as well as a writer for theater and film. In *The Writer on Her Work*, she has commissioned and edited a body of work reflecting her special interest in women and creativity. Among the films she has written or produced are *Virginia Woolf: The Moment Whole* and *Thomas Eakins: A Motion Portrait*. She lives in both Los Angeles and New York, serving as media adviser to the Rockefeller Foundation as well as teacher of creative writing at the California Institute of the Arts.

THE WRITER
ON HER WORK

EDITED AND WITH
AN INTRODUCTION BY

JANET STERNBURG

Published by VIRAGO PRESS Limited 1992
20–23 Mandela Street, Camden Town, London NW1 0HQ

First published in two volumes in the United States by
W.W. Norton & Co., 1981 and 1991

*A CIP catalogue record for this book is available from the
British Library*

Scanned and Filmset by J&L Composition Ltd, Filey, North Yorkshire
Printed in Great Britain by Cox & Wyman Ltd, Reading, Berkshire

CONTENTS

ACKNOWLEDGMENTS

"My Vocation" by Natalia Ginzburg, reprinted from *The Little Virtues* by Natalia Ginzburg, copyright © 1962 by Giulio Einaudi s.p.a., Turin, translation copyright © 1985 by Dick Davis, published by Seaver Books, New York, 1986, and reprinted with permission of Seaver Books and Carcanet Press Limited.

"*One* Child of One's Own: A Meaningful Digression within the Work(s)" by Alice Walker, copyright © 1978, 1980 Alice Walker.

"Blood and Guts: The Tricky Problem of Being a Woman Writer in the Late Twentieth Century" by Erica Jong, copyright © 1980 Erica Mann Jong.

"Why I Write" by Joan Didion, copyright © 1976 by Joan Didion. First appeared in the *New York Times Book Review*. Reprinted by permission of the Wallace Literary Agency, Inc.

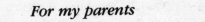

For my parents

JANET STERNBURG

THE WRITER HERSELF:
AN INTRODUCTION

I'M drawn back to a room from my childhood—the back room
of my aunt's apartment. When my parents and I visited, I used to
vanish into that room. My means of escape was the typewriter,
an old manual that sat on a desk in the back room. It belonged to
my aunt, but she had long since left it for the adjoining room, the
kitchen. She had once wanted to write, but as the eldest of a
large and troubled first-generation American family, she had
other claims on her energies as well as proscriptions to contend
with: class, gender, and situation joined to make her feel
unworthy of literature.

I now know that I inherited some of her proscriptions, but the
back room at age nine was a place of freedom. There I could
perform that significant act: I could close the door. Certainly I
felt peculiar on leaving the warm and buzzing room of conversation, with its charge of familial love and invasion. But it wasn't
the living room I needed: it was the writing room, which now
comes back to me with its metal table, its stack of white paper
that did not diminish between my visits. I would try my hand at
poems; I would also construct elaborate multiple-choice tests.
"A child is an artist when, seeing a tree at dusk, she (a) climbs it
(b) sketches it (c) goes home and describes it in her notebook."
And another (possibly imagined) one: "A child is an artist when,
visiting her relatives, she (a) goes down to the street to play (b)
talks with her family and becomes a part of them (c) goes into
the back room to write."

Oh my. Buried in those self-administered tests were the seeds
of what, years later, made me stop writing. Who could possibly
respond correctly to so severe an inquisition? Nonetheless, that
room was essential to me. I remember sitting at the desk and

feeling my excitement start to build; soon I'd touch the type-writer keys, soon I'd be back in my own world. Although I felt strange and isolated, I was beginning to speak, through writing. And if I chose, I could throw out what I'd done that day; there was no obligation to show my words to anyone.

Looking back now, I feel sad at so constrained a sense of freedom, so defensive a stance: retreat behind a closed door. Much later, when I returned to writing after many silent years, I believed that the central act was to open that door, to make writing into something which would not stand in opposition to others. I imagined a room at the heart of a house, and life in its variety flowing in and out. Later still I came to see that I continued to value separation and privacy. I began to realize that once again I'd constructed a test: the true writer either retreats and pays the price of isolation from the human stream or opens the door and pays the price of exposure to too many diverse currents. Now I've come to believe that there is no central act; instead there is a central struggle, ongoing, which is to retain control over the door—to shut it when necessary, open it at other times—and to retain the freedom to give up that control, and experiment with the room as porous. I've also come to believe that my harsh childhood testing was an attempt at self-definition—but one made in isolation, with no knowledge of living writers. In place of a more expansive range of choices that acquaintance, especially with working women writers, could have provided, I substituted the notion of a single criterion for an artist. That view has altered with becoming a woman and a writer. As part of that change, I've wanted to know how other women came to write and how they see their lives and their work. And so this book began because I needed to read it.

As I write this introduction, I think now of the rich array of the contributors: of, among others, Jan Morris, once a man with a shelf of books under her earlier identity as James, and now a woman whose books go on multiplying; of Natalia Ginzburg, forced into confinement by the Fascists during the Second World War and, many years later, serving as senator in the Italian Parliament; of Bharati Mukherjee, travelling from one continent to make her home in another and writing about the "unsettled magma between two worlds"; of Margaret Walker, also traveling a long span that reaches from her 1920's girlhood in America's Deep South across a career as distinguished African-American woman of letters, who says in these pages that "it has always been my feeling that writing must come out of living."

By appreciating the variety and depth of experience in these essays, I don't, of course, mean to correlate the fact of interesting lives with the ability to create literature. But my desire to elicit that range did inform the choices I made in commissioning the essays in this volume, as did my admiration for the work of the individual authors. The diversity of writers suggests another hallmark: my intent has been to foster accounts in which the central themes of the making of one's work and one's self are refracted through personal sensibilities, and are expressed through the human, concrete particulars that are the materials of literature. The choices have been informed, too, by my decision to include writers from many countries, with the hope that multiple voices, side by side, will suggest how the commonalities of women's experience can only become richer through the cross-fertilization of differences.

In the future, a woman writer may well feel released from the question of gender and its effect on her work, but I believe that the experience of her predecessors will be telling. Until recent years, however, it has been hard to get a clear view of that experience. Women writers in the past have written about themselves and their work, but sparsely; often the material has had to be gleaned from memoirs, diaries, letters, fiction, and poetry. Poems, for example, yield instances of the writer on her vocation: Anne Bradstreet in seventeenth-century colonial America wrote poems about the vicissitudes of being a woman writer, as did Anne Finch, Countess of Winchilsea and, in the nineteenth century, Emily Dickinson and Elizabeth Barrett Browning. We have memoirs, diaries, and letters by George Sand, Simone de Beauvoir, Colette, George Eliot, Virginia Woolf; we have even more oblique sources such as Gertrude Stein's *The Autobiography of Alice B. Toklas*. And, certainly, scholars have been working with the papers of women writers both known and obscure, and finding passages that illuminate the art and situation of that writer and, by extension, of other women writers. Nonetheless, a fact remains: we have had very little by women that intentionally and directly addresses the subject of their own art.

To be sure, we have had stereotypical images of the "woman writer": recluse, sufferer, woman in mauve velvet on a chaise, woman who flees the stifling rooms of her father's house, adventuress, "free" woman of multiple love affairs, paragon of productivity, destroyer of others, more often of herself. The images are all too familiar—away with them! In their place, I suggest we picture a woman (of whatever age) sitting (at a desk, on a bench in the playground, on a bus ...) with paper in front of her and a pen in her hand. No more. *But no less*. That woman is asking herself questions. They are the questions of all writers— form and craft, value and meaning, relationship and identity. One that reverberates throughout this collection is "How do I come to be here?" Each writer in this book is taking stock; that is, she is making a sort of inventory of what she has, of her means, so as to know what she has to give. The writers in this book refuse to define themselves into a single formulation; instead, they embrace many selves, many relations.

The women here write of the necessity to explore these relations: to traverse the mutable ground that lies between one culture and another, between oneself and others, as well as between a writer and her vocation. A number of the writers convey the experience of having been displaced by history, and the impact upon their writing of a life lived in several landscapes. Mukherjee, crossing the distance between India and the United States, writes, "My literary agenda begins by acknowledging that America has transformed me. It does not end until I show how I (and the hundreds of thousands like me) have transformed America." In these pages, too, we are given images from the high Western European tradition, intensified for people sent into exile: Elizabeth Jolley evokes her father listening to Schubert's *Lieder*, shading his hand over his eyes to hide tears. But these writers refuse the lure of nostalgia. Instead, with Mukherjee, they embrace as their subject "transformation—not preservation". For Toni Cade Bambara, "writing is one of the ways I participate in the transformation—one of the ways I practice the commitment to explore bodies of knowledge for the usable truths they yield". Several of the essays here refer also to the relationship of writer as witness, or scribe, or bridge between generations: conveyors all of the truths of others. Ursula Le Guin in her poem/ essay taps the sources of world cultures; when she invokes Aphrodite the Maker, Spider Grandmother, and Coyote Woman, she is writing not to appropriate the cultures to which these references belong but rather to find kinship among an extensive range of understandings.

What relations are necessary, these essays also ask, for a writer to belong to herself and also to others? In accounts of becoming a writer, one often finds that a child has been estranged in one way or another—by loss, illness, or other isolating occurrences— from what is taken to be normal life. This setting apart, so influential in a writer's childhood, acquires a different meaning for an adult. On the one hand, it remains necessary; on the other hand, setting apart can be hazardous in that it may also mean withdrawal from an equally necessary involvement with daily life. This dilemma of the creative life has long had particular meaning for women who have traditionally found it difficult to negotiate the relationship between *apart* and *a part*. There is such poignancy in these lines of Elizabeth Jolley's: "The best time for me to write is when people are sleeping. I am not needed in their dreams."

Certainly, this relationship of self to others takes on particular acuity for the writer who is also a mother. Remembering the period of her life after the birth of her first baby, Anne Tyler writes, "Even if I had found the time to write, I wouldn't have had the insides. I felt drained; too much care and feeling were being drawn out of me." That sense of external and internal besiegement by the claims of others is a note that resonates in this book, as does the choice (and the necessity!) to answer responsibly and lovingly to those claims. "Sometimes, the only quiet and private place where I could write a sonnet was in the bathroom", writes Margaret Walker, "because that was the only room where the door could be locked and no one would intrude … I have written mostly at night in my adult life and especially since I have been married, because I was determined not to neglect my family; so I cooked every meal daily, washed dishes and dirty clothes, and nursed sick babies."

I continue to be touched by a passage from a little-known memoir, Katherine Butler Hathaway's *The Little Locksmith* (1943):

> Although every serious person is expected to feel a responsibility toward his work as well as toward the people he loves, there is a point beyond which his devotion to his work cannot go without arousing the antagonism and jealousy of the people who love him and whom he loves. And, as everyone knows, Art is jealous too. This conflict can be as tragic as a civil war, because it is a war of the heart, between people who love each other.

I find the quote particularly apt for this book not only because the writers here refer to the conflict but also because many of them describe the fray through the lens of time, looking back at periods in their lives and in the general culture when the discord was particularly acute. In place of despair, they tell of the variety of strategies that they employed to put an end to that war of the heart, not by a victory, one side over the other, or even by the stalemate of a truce, but by the establishing of just relations. Reflecting on her dual commitment to her family and to her writing, Anne Tyler says, "It seems to me that since I've had children, I've grown richer and deeper. They may have slowed down my writing for a while, but when I did write, I had more of a self to speak from." That growth of the writer's self, in continual calibration with life's other demands, seems to me to be at the heart of this book.

Constant here, and unswerving, is the writer's commitment to her vocation. It is reassuring to hear so practiced a writer as Margaret Atwood say, "It never gets any easier". Atwood also speaks of writing as a craft, one that is "acquired through the apprenticeship system, but you choose your own teachers". The writers in this book have made their vocations from paths they have hewn themselves. Their teachers include a variety of relations, among them mothers, daughters, grandmothers, husbands, friends, colleagues, remembered figures from the past, mentors urging one into one's future, as well as the writer's own self, reexamining and renewing her understandings.

For me, writing something down was the only road out.

Anne Tyler

For all the writers in this book, writing is necessary for survival; it is "the road out". That road is wide and long enough to accommodate many travellers; what propels them, though, differs from writer to writer. Mary Gordon sees writing as a way out of inauthenticity; through the practice of her art, she changes from a girl who wanted to please by writing from a distant perspective about exotic adventures—a classic province of male writers—to a woman who writes to preserve the 'complexity of the quotidian' that she values. Alice Walker sees writing as rescuing her from "the sin and inconvenience of violence"—out of the impotence of being assaulted by conditions that enrage her and into words that release her feelings and help to change those conditions. For Joan Didion, writing is release from the buzz of her mind. Images come to her without explanation and refuse to go away; characters also come unbidden. "I write entirely to find out what I'm thinking, what I'm looking at, what I see and what it means. What I want and what I fear." Like Walker's, Didion's writing is an answer to violence— but here the violence is exclusively inner; not to understand these apparitions might lead to violence against oneself. Maxine Hong Kingston speaks of having to make "trails of words". In her essay, she hopes to join a collective vision larger than what has conditioned her. Her way to that vision, however, is not by willing it but by surrendering to it. The visions come from the thick growth of all she is and has been; she must find the trail and follow it.

For Anita Desai, writing is the way back, a means of return to childhood experiences both to discern their deeper truths and to recover a landscape that once had nurtured her: "words spun the thread that led me back ... words were the bridge and became the web." Ursula Le Guin, finding herself in the darkness, lost, "where the road turned/and divided ... took the way that didn't say./I followed/myself." All of these writers have moved through a route that has taken them from imitation and the need for approval (as in Diane Johnson's evocation of "the ghost of Henry James glaring over my shoulder") to a reckoning with the validity of their experience and a coming into their own inimitable territory: the authenticity of their writing. "When I write stories", says Natalia Ginzburg, "I am like someone who is in her own country, walking along streets that she has known since she was a child, between walls and trees that are hers." For Erica Jong, writing leads her away from voices inside her that say "turn back, you'll die if you venture too far." One metaphor in Jong's essay is exploration: curiosity that propels the venture and willingness to search out the unknown.

When an individual writer tells of her day-to-day struggles, what we're seeing in operation is a person claiming her original impulse and carrying it forward—knowing that as she does so, she commits herself to change. Sartre once called for "a more conscious artist ... who, by reflecting on his art, would try to endow it with his condition as a man". That quest which was previously arrogated by men has been taken on, with full intent, by women.

In this transitional time, the notion of a world split by gender diminishes everyone. Whether women are relegated to a partial sphere or whether we appropriate it, we lose encompassing meaning. While writing as a vocation is understood here through the focus of writers who are female, there is salutary debate in these pages about whether gender does or should influence the creation of art. To my mind, there is also summation in Diane Johnson's recognition, both complex and transparently obvious, that "if you are a woman writer, you will naturally see things from a female perspective, your experience having been shaped that way ..." But she warns against any attempt to reduce that experience by seeing it as limited, or special: "I object to things that concern half the human race (all the human race really) being relegated to the status of political issue instead of being seen as an aspect of human experience of concern and interest to everybody." The concerns of women writers speak to the ways in which lives and art transform and enrich one another. As women continue to bring our perspective to this exchange, we extend beyond ourselves and illuminate new points of convergence.

I think again about how I began *The Writer on Her Work*: conscious of changes in my life and in the world, I wanted to read writing that not only explores the many dimensions of change but is also transformative in its own right. I think too of Natalia Ginzburg's beautiful image: how, as a young woman, she saw a cart on the street one day bearing a mirror whose surface was tilted up to reflect sky and clouds. That image of the mirror initially evoked a vision of what might be possible, helping to release her from strictures she had placed upon herself and her writing. During a later period of difficulty, the mirror became dark to Ginzburg. But I believe that in the years that followed she let its metaphor deepen until it eventually reflected a view of art as compounded from a "mixture of pride, irony, physical tenderness, of imagination and memory, of clarity and obscurity". In place of a single image, however luminous it must once have been within its frame, we see instead the necessity for a more complex vision.

There is a sense in many of these essays of women comprehending themselves as amalgams of experiences, some that fit together in a clear trajectory, others that diverge or collide. "She tends to the plural", writes Ursula Le Guin: "I, for example, am Ursula: Miss Ursula Kroeber/Mrs. then Ms. Le Guin/Ursula K. Le Guin; this latter is/'the writer' but who were/who are, the others? She is the writer/at their work." There is a tone of playfulness here, a pleasure in sliding under the wire of definitions and in accepting life's revisions, that might not have been possible a decade or so ago. To me, that pleasure feels related to a relaxation that has been arrived at because hard-won changes of past years have allowed many women to shrug from their shoulders the burden of rigidly imposed identity.

This understanding of one's self as a fullness of many selves gives us a new plenitude. In answer to her question "What are they doing,/those plurals of her?", Le Guin responds, I believe, for all the writers in this book:

Her work, I really think her work
is finding what her real work is
and doing it
her work, her own work
her being human,
her being in the world.

JOAN DIDION

WHY I WRITE

This essay is adapted from a Regents' Lecture delivered at the
University of California at Berkeley.

O F course I stole the title for this talk, from George Orwell.
One reason I stole it was that I like the sound of the words: Why
I Write. There you have three short unambiguous words that
share a sound, and the sound they share is this:

I

I

I

In many ways writing is the act of saying *I*, of imposing oneself
upon other people, of saying *listen to me, see it my way, change
your mind*. It's an aggressive, even a hostile act. You can disguise
its aggressiveness all you want with veils of subordinate clauses
and qualifiers and tentative subjunctives, with ellipses and
evasions—with the whole manner of intimating rather than
claiming, of alluding rather than stating—but there's no getting
around the fact that setting words on paper is the tactic of a
secret bully, an invasion, an imposition of the writer's sensibility
on the reader's most private space.

I stole the title not only because the words sounded right but
because they seemed to sum up, in a no-nonsense way, all I have
to tell you. Like many writers I have only this one "subject," this
one "area": the act of writing. I can bring you no reports from
any other front. I may have other interests: I am "interested," for
example, in marine biology, but I don't flatter myself that you
would come out to hear me talk about it. I am not a scholar. I am
not in the least an intellectual, which is not to say that when I
hear the word "intellectual" I reach for my gun, but only to say
that I do not think in abstracts. During the years when I was an
undergraduate at Berkeley I tried, with a kind of hopeless

late-adolescent energy, to buy some temporary visa into the
world of ideas, to forge for myself a mind that could deal with
the abstract.

In short I tried to think. I failed. My attention veered inexor-
ably back to the specific, to the tangible, to what was generally
considered, by everyone I knew then and for that matter have
known since, the peripheral. I would try to contemplate the
Hegelian dialectic and would find myself concentrating instead
on a flowering pear tree outside my window and the particular
way the petals fell on my floor. I would try to read linguistic
theory and would find myself wondering instead if the lights
were on in the bevatron up the hill. When I say that I was
wondering if the lights were on in the bevatron you might
immediately suspect, if you deal in ideas at all, that I was
registering the bevatron as a political symbol, thinking in
shorthand about the military-industrial complex and its role in
the university community, but you would be wrong. I was only
wondering if the lights were on in the bevatron, and how they
looked. A physical fact.

I had trouble graduating from Berkeley, not because of this
inability to deal with ideas—I was majoring in English, and I
could locate the house-and-garden imagery in *The Portrait of a
Lady* as well as the next person, "imagery" being by definition
the kind of specific that got my attention—but simply because I
had neglected to take a course in Milton. For reasons which now
sound baroque I needed a degree by the end of that summer, and
the English department finally agreed, if I would come down
from Sacramento every Friday and talk about the cosmology of
Paradise Lost, to certify me proficient in Milton. I did this. Some
Fridays I took the Greyhound bus, other Fridays I caught the
Southern Pacific's City of San Francisco on the last leg of its
transcontinental trip. I can no longer tell you whether Milton
put the sun or the earth at the center of his universe in *Paradise
Lost*, the central question of at least one century and a topic
about which I wrote 10,000 words that summer, but I can still
recall the exact rancidity of the butter in the City of San
Francisco's dining car, and the way the tinted windows on the
Greyhound bus cast the oil refineries around Carquinez Straits

into a grayed and obscurely sinister light. In short my attention was always on the periphery, on what I could see and taste and touch, on the butter, and the Greyhound bus. During those years I was traveling on what I knew to be a very shaky passport, forged papers: I knew that I was no legitimate resident in any world of ideas. I knew I couldn't think. All I knew then was what I couldn't do. All I knew then was what I wasn't, and it took me some years to discover what I was.

Which was a writer.

By which I mean not a "good" writer or a "bad" writer but simply a writer, a person whose most absorbed and passionate hours are spent arranging words on pieces of paper. Had my credentials been in order I would never have become a writer. Had I been blessed with even limited access to my own mind there would have been no reason to write. I write entirely to find out what I'm thinking, what I'm looking at, what I see and what it means. What I want and what I fear. Why did the oil refineries around Carquinez Straits seem sinister to me in the summer of 1956? Why have the night lights in the bevatron burned in my mind for twenty years? *What is going on in these pictures in my mind?*

When I talk about pictures in my mind I am talking, quite specifically, about images that shimmer around the edges. There used to be an illustration in every elementary psychology book showing a cat drawn by a patient in varying stages of schizophrenia. This cat had a shimmer around it. You could see the molecular structure breaking down at the very edges of the cat: the cat became the background and the background the cat, everything interacting, exchanging ions. People on hallucinogens describe the same perception of objects. I'm not a schizophrenic, nor do I take hallucinogens, but certain images do shimmer for me. Look hard enough, and you can't miss the shimmer. It's there. You can't think too much about these pictures that shimmer. You just lie low and let them develop. You stay quiet. You don't talk to many people and you keep your nervous system from shorting out and you try to locate the cat in the shimmer, the grammar in the picture.

Just as I meant "shimmer" literally I mean "grammar" literally.

Grammar is a piano I play by ear, since I seem to have been out
of school the year the rules were mentioned. All I know about
grammar is its infinite power. To shift the structure of a sentence
alters the meaning of that sentence, as definitely and inflexibly as
the position of a camera alters the meaning of the object
photographed. Many people know about camera angles now, but
not so many know about sentences. The arrangement of the
words matters, and the arrangement you want can be found in
the picture in your mind. The picture dictates the arrangement.
The picture dictates whether this will be a sentence with or
without clauses, a sentence that ends hard or a dying-fall
sentence, long or short, active or passive. The picture tells you
how to arrange the words and the arrangement of the words tells
you, or tells me, what's going on in the picture. *Nota bene*:

It tells you.

You don't tell it.

Let me show you what I mean by pictures in the mind. I began
Play It as It Lays just as I have begun each of my novels, with no
notion of "character" or "plot" or even "incident." I had only
two pictures in my mind, more about which later, and a
technical intention, which was to write a novel so elliptical and
fast that it would be over before you noticed it, a novel so fast
that it would scarcely exist on the page at all. About the pictures:
the first was of white space. Empty space. This was clearly the
picture that dictated the narrative intention of the book—a book
in which anything that happened would happen off the page, a
"white" book to which the reader would have to bring his or her
own bad dreams—and yet this picture told me no "story,"
suggested no situation. The second picture did. This second
picture was of something actually witnessed. A young woman
with long hair and a short white halter dress walks through the
casino at the Riviera in Las Vegas at one in the morning. She
crosses the casino alone and picks up a house telephone. I watch
her because I have heard her paged, and recognize her name: she
is a minor actress I see around Los Angeles from time to time, in
places like Jax and once in a gynecologist's office in the Beverly
Hills Clinic, but have never met. I know nothing about her. Who
is paging her? Why is she here to be paged? How exactly did she

come to this? It was precisely this moment in Las Vegas that made *Play It as It Lays* begin to tell itself to me, but the moment appears in the novel only obliquely, in a chapter which begins:

"Maria made a list of things she would never do. She would never: walk through the Sands or Caesar's alone after midnight. She would never: ball at a party, do S-M unless she wanted to, borrow furs from Abe Lipsey, deal. She would never: carry a Yorkshire in Beverly Hills."

That is the beginning of the chapter and that is also the end of the chapter, which may suggest what I meant by "white space."

I recall having a number of pictures in my mind when I began the novel I just finished, *A Book of Common Prayer*. As a matter of fact one of these pictures was of that bevatron I mentioned, although I would be hard put to tell you a story in which nuclear energy figures. Another was a newspaper photograph or a hijacked 707 burning on the desert in the Middle East. Another was the night view from a room in which I once spent a week with paratyphoid, a hotel room on the Colombian coast. My husband and I seemed to be on the Colombian coast representing the United States of America at a film festival (I recall invoking the name "Jack Valenti" a lot, as if its reiteration could make me well), and it was a bad place to have fever, not only because my indisposition offended our hosts but because every night in this hotel the generator failed. The lights went out. The elevator stopped. My husband would go to the event of the evening and make excuses for me and would stay alone in this hotel room, in the dark. I remember standing at the window trying to call Bogotá (the telephone seemed to work on the same principle as the generator) and watching the night wind come up and wondering what I was doing eleven degrees off the equator with a fever of 103. The view from that window definitely figures in *A Book of Common Prayer*, as does the burning 707, and yet none of these pictures told me the story I needed.

The picture that did, the picture that shimmered and made these other images coalesce, was the Panama airport at 6 A.M. I was in this airport only once, on a plane to Bogotá that stopped for an hour to refuel, but the way it looked that morning

remained superimposed on everything I saw until the day I
finished *A Book of Common Prayer*. I lived in that airport for
several years. I can still feel the hot air when I step off the plane,
can see the heat already rising off the tarmac at 6 A.M. I can feel
my skirt damp and wrinkled on my legs. I can feel the asphalt
stick to my sandals. I remember the big tail of a Pan American
plane floating motionless down at the end of the tarmac. I
remember the sound of a slot machine in the waiting room. I
could tell you that I remember a particular woman in the airport,
an American woman, a *norteameritana*, a thin *norteamericana*
about forty who wore a big square emerald in lieu of a wedding
ring, but there was no such woman there.

I put this woman in the airport later. I made this woman up,
just as I later made up a country to put the airport in, and a
family to run the country. This woman in the airport is neither
catching a plane nor meeting one. She is ordering tea in the
airport coffee shop. In fact she is not simply "ordering" tea but
insisting that the water be boiled, in front of her, for twenty
minutes. Why is this woman in this airport? Why is she going
nowhere, where has she been? Where did she get that big
emerald? What derangement, or disassociation, makes her
believe that her will to see the water boiled can possibly prevail?

"She had been going to one airport or another for four
months, one could see it, looking at the visas on her passport. All
those airports where Charlotte Douglas's passport had been
stamped would have looked alike. Sometimes the sign on the
tower would say "Bienvenidos" and sometimes the sign on the
tower would say "Bienvenue," some places were wet and hot
and others dry and hot, but at each of these airports the pastel
concrete walls would rust and stain and the swamp off the
runway would be littered with the fuselages of cannibalized
Fairchild F-227's and the water would need boiling.

"I knew why Charlotte went to the airport even if Victor did
not.

"I knew about airports."

These lines appear about halfway through *A Book of Common
Prayer*, but I wrote them during the second week I worked on
the book, long before I had any idea where Charlotte Douglas

had been or why she went to airports. Until I wrote these lines I had no character called Victor" in mind: the necessity for mentioning a name, and the name "Victor," occurred to me as I wrote the sentence. *I knew why Charlotte went to the airport* sounded incomplete. *I knew why Charlotte went to the airport even if Victor did not* carried a little more narrative drive. Most important of all, until I wrote these lines I did not know who "I" was, who was telling the story. I had intended until that that the "I" be no more than the voice of the author, a nineteenth-century omniscient narrator. But there it was:

"I knew why Charlotte went to the airport even if Victor did not.

"I knew about airports."

This "I" was the voice of no author in my house. This "I" was someone who not only knew why Charlotte went to the airport but also knew someone called "Victor." Who was Victor? Who was this narrator? Why was this narrator telling me this story? Let me tell you one thing about why writers write: had I known the answer to any of these questions I would never have needed to write a novel.

ANITA DESAI

A FIRE HAD TO BE LIT

I suppose I began to write *Fire on the Mountain* when I was eight years old and taken to Kasauli for the summer—even if I did not put down a word on paper then. At that time I was not the narrator of a book, but the source of one. That summer I was suspected by my mother of not being well or strong and requiring special attention, and was therefore kept mostly at home which was, for the summer, a large, square stone house on the hillside below the town. While my brother and older sisters roamed the upper ridges in search of adventures, I played by myself in the garden or wandered in the cornfields, pine groves, and apricot orchards immediately surrounding the house. Although I missed some grand and rather terrifying adventures, I believe it was because of this imposed isolation that I absorbed my surroundings, mulled over them and retained impressions at their most pure and vivid. I was not dissipating them by sharing them with anyone, or diluting them by giving them only half my attention. The flash of a silvery langur's fur through the foliage, the odor of the dry pine needles on the hillsides, and the feel of the stones and pieces of bark I played with in my solitary games sank into me indelibly: they sank in so deep that I lost sight of them and forgot them.

They stirred to life again when some twenty years later I found myself living in Chandigarh (which had not existed in 1945), and going up to Kasauli for holidays once more. This time it was my children who were exploring the hillsides, and through them I relived those earlier, almost forgotten experiences of sliding down a hillside slippery with pine needles, driving away a band of langurs that had descended on our zinc roof, gazing at the smoke from a forest fire and wondering if it would draw much closer. Like seeds that had been buried deep in the soil and stirred to life on feeling a shower of rain and the coming of the right season, the memories became living experiences once again.

While walking along the Kasauli Mall I would sometimes stop by the fence to look down the steep hillside at a small village below, its haystacks and cattle and stony paths, its small population of laborers going about with their backs bent under sheaves of grass, sickles tucked in at the waist. I wondered then if it was this village—or one nearby—where an acquaintance of my mother's had been done to death, a woman I had seen perhaps half a dozen times during my childhood, and since then quite forgotten. Miss R. was a spinster lady who taught, I think, in one of the women's colleges in Delhi; she had sometimes visited my mother in order to pour out her woes to a sympathetic listener. I am afraid she met with little sympathy from me. Like my father and brother and sisters, I found her tiny desiccated figure and astonishingly loud, braying voice utterly ludicrous and would run away, choking with laughter, when I heard her voice ring out at the gate. She was afflicted with a voice no one could bear; I doubt if she had any friends. Later, she left Delhi; my mother told me she was involved in social work in a village near Kasauli. I think we received a few letters, telling of her hardships, her lack of money, her inability to do anything for the ignorant and stubborn villagers. Still later, the news came that she had been brutally assaulted and murdered by a villager, who resented her presence and her proselytizing. We were shocked. Then we forgot. She faded away.

On leaving the north and moving to Bombay, I felt the need to recapture that landscape which seemed essential to my survival—if I were not to die from the onslaught of a great and abrasive city, its unrelieved ugliness, squalor, and noise. I sat

down at my desk and set myself to recreating the sounds and
smells and sights of the Kasauli hills. It was my belief in the
magic power of words that made me feel I could do so through
an act of intense concentration—and replace my actual presence
there. To do that, I had to send my eight-year-old self out into
the hills again, wearing a straw hat that had slipped onto my back
and chafed my shoulders, my feet in open sandals feeling the
white dust and stubbing against the stones again. That child, its
solitude, became the focal point of the book.

I had experienced that summer and those hills in solitude, and
solitude became its natural theme. Although I had lost that sense
of isolation on later holidays there, I recalled a woman who used
to live on top of the hill above the cottage we rented, a Mrs. S.,
whom I had not known personally but knew of and whose gray
melancholy presence had struck me greatly. I used to see her
going for walks alone; occasionally on passing her house, I heard
her playing her piano, meditatively and compellingly. I was later
told of her lonely death that she seemed to have willed upon
herself. She joined the small sunburnt child straying on the
hillside, as the second of my two characters.

Then, I was halfway through my book, still trying to discover
why these two characters—the melancholy gray lady and the
cricket-like child—were where they were, when I saw a gray,
indistinct figure looming over the horizon, as insubstantial as a
wisp of smoke from a forest fire. For a while, I could neither
recognize it nor understand its presence in my book. Then,
when I began to describe it, I gave a start of astonishment as I
recognized Miss R. It was her ghost that had climbed up the
hillside onto the Mall and accosted me. I heard her voice ring
out, shattering the silence that enclosed my two characters, in a
scream for attention. In my state of shock, I forgot to laugh; in
fact, I found I could not laugh any more; I saw now that she was
not laughable at all, she was tragic. Although she had played a
minute, indeed minuscule role in my life until then, and I had

not thought about her in thirty years, she must have remained buried in my subconscious. To lay her ghost, to exorcise her unspeakable past, it was necessary to write about her. My memory of Miss R. was flawed; I saw her and remembered her from the viewpoint of a child unwilling to give her any time or sympathy—I was not capable then of either. It was therefore necessary to go back to my spare memories of her; attempt to understand and picture her wretched existence and unthinkable death—in order to arrive at what seemed to be the truth.

These characters could not exist in a vacuum; they could not float in space. They had to be provided with a background, and it had to be so real that it could be touched, heard, and felt. Kasauli provided that: sitting in a flat in Bombay and looking out over the slums smothered in city smog, I was nevertheless in touch with a different landscape, sunburnt and stark; words spun the threads that led me back to it, words were the bridge and became the web. The landscape could not possibly be just a background; it was too powerful to be merely that. Surely that twisted pine tree with two branches like outflung arms against the sky had some meaning ... the kite floating on currents of air through the gorges and silent chasms was symbol of some mystery that I could not understand, but invited me to delve into it and discover its significance, or at least proclaim its presence.

There were other elements that went into the making of the jigsaw puzzle, some vague and others definite; the element of terror that is never absent from even the most sunlit places of childhood (Flannery O'Connor: "Anybody who has survived childhood has enough information about life to last him the rest of his days"). The research at the Pasteur Institute that I had heard about as a child was connected with the horrors of snakebite and rabies, and became very real when we later lived in a cottage that overlooked the gorge into which the Pasteur Institute emptied its chutes and from which we could see its prison-like walls and its blackened smokestacks. ... A nighttime

walk down a shadow-patterned road when we children tried to
terrify each other by telling ghost stories ... the small white graves
overgrown with grass in the British cemetery. ... Also the
impression, a lasting one, made on me by Mrs. Ramsay in *To the
Lighthouse* and the clinging charm of Sei Shonagon's *Pillow
Book*. ... The writing of the book became a curious mingling of the
real and the remembered and the imagined—as every novel is. It
is, after all, as E. M. Forster said, "won by the mind from matter"
and contains elements of both. The two can be seen as locked in
combat or in harmony, but the right proportions have to be found
in order to balance the whole. If the book is to be strong, effective,
and meaningful, then the gaps between these elements, between
the real and the imagined worlds, the objective and the subjective
attitudes, the extrovert and the introvert elements, have to be
closed up; the two must mesh together leaving no gaps through
which credulity could drain. Having built oneself such a container, it might surprise one to see, when lowering it into those
depths of memory, or swinging it through the free space of
imagination, what it might catch and net.

Having pinned down my butterfly with my nib, I was not
finished with it; I had still to see it through the press, correct
proofs, finally be faced with the sight of it in a bookshop, available
to all. It had many incarnations: an English edition to begin with;
then an American edition that carried the picture of a black witch
on the cover; a paperback edition that displayed a bright hoopoe,
a fly-swatter, and a landscape that never was; then translations in
which I lost sight of the original, and that became originals in
themselves. ... It was read and received reviews. I was questioned
about it. Readers were disturbed: what did it all mean? Was it a real
fire or a symbolic one? Why did the child start it? Did the old lady
die, or faint—"or what?" Since I was responsible for it, I had to
defend it. "Don't you see?" I replied. "Everyone in that book is
living an illusion—their lives are built on illusions. To be rid of
them, a fire had to be lit and only the child was pure enough to
light it. Everything had to be burnt away in order to reduce it to
ash and reveal the truth." I was surprised by my own explanation:

it had not occurred to me till I gave it that it was one. Certainly it was not my intention when I began to write that book but, to my relief, it fitted; it had been fortuitous but it had turned out right—one of those instances of stumbling upon the truth rather than pursuing and capturing it.

*   *   *

These final and richly satisfying explanations never occur to a writer while writing the book. Such verbalizations of the conflicts, of the disappointments and pride, of satisfaction and dismay, come much later and serve chiefly to soothe one's conscience, to act as a healing, mending plaster upon a wound, to persuade one that time has not been thrown away and life not wasted. While writing one is only aware of the compulsion to write, barely understood but nevertheless powerfully felt and of which John Updike spoke when he said he wrote a particular novel "because the rhythm of my life and my 'oeuvre' demanded it, not to placate hallucinatory critical voices."

That is the very answer one might extract from a spider, if answer it could give on being asked to justify its web. It spins because spinning is what is demanded of it by the rhythm of its life, and its oeuvre.

ANNE TYLER

STILL JUST WRITING

WHILE I was painting the downstairs hall I thought of a novel to write. Really I just thought of a character; he more or less wandered into my mind, wearing a beard and a broad-brimmed leather hat. I figured that if I sat down and organized this character on paper, a novel would grow up around him. But it was March and the children's spring vacation began the next day, so I waited.

After spring vacation the children went back to school, but the dog got worms. It was a little complicated at the vet's and I lost a day. By then it was Thursday; Friday is the only day I can buy the groceries, pick up new cedar chips for the gerbils, scrub the bathrooms. I waited till Monday. Still, that left me four good weeks in April to block out the novel.

By May I was ready to start actually writing, but I had to do it in patches. There was the follow-up treatment at the vet, and then a half-day spent trailing the dog with a specimen tin so the lab could be sure the treatment had really worked. There were visits from the washing machine repairman and the Davey tree man, not to mention briefer interruptions by the meter reader, five Jehovah's Witnesses, and two Mormons. People telephoned wanting to sell me permanent light bulbs and waterproof basements. An Iranian cousin of my husband's had a baby; then the cousin's uncle died; then the cousin's mother decided to go home to Iran and needed to know where to buy a black American coat before she left. There *are* no black American coats; don't Americans wear mourning? I told her no, but I checked around at all the department stores anyway because she didn't speak English. Then I wrote chapters one and two. I had planned to work till three-thirty every day, but it was a month of early quittings: once for the children's dental appointment, once for the cat's rabies shot, once for our older daughter's orthopedist, and twice for her gymnastic meets. Sitting on the bleachers in the school gymnasium, I told myself I could always use this in a novel someplace, but I couldn't really picture writing a novel about twenty little girls in leotards trying to walk the length of a wooden beam without falling off. By the time I'd written chapter three, it was Memorial Day and the children were home again.

I knew I shouldn't expect anything from June. School was finished then and camp hadn't yet begun. I put the novel away. I closed down my mind and planted some herbs and played cribbage with the children. Then on the 25th, we drove one child to a sleep-away camp in Virginia and entered the other in a day camp, and I was ready to start work again. First I had to take my car in for repairs and the mechanics lost it, but I didn't get diverted. I sat in the garage on a folding chair while they hunted my car all one afternoon, and I hummed a calming tune and tried to remember what I'd planned to do next in my novel. Or even what the novel was about, for that matter. My character wandered in again in his beard and his broad-brimmed hat. He looked a little pale and knuckly, like someone scrabbling at a cliff edge so as not to fall away entirely.

I had high hopes for July, but it began with a four-day weekend, and on Monday night we had a long-distance call from our daughter's camp in Virginia. She was seriously ill in a Charlottesville hospital. We left our youngest with friends and drove three hours in a torrent of rain. We found our daughter frightened and crying, and another child (the only other child I knew in all of Virginia) equally frightened and crying down in the emergency room with possible appendicitis, so I spent that night alternating between a chair in the pediatric wing and a chair in the emergency room. By morning, it had begun to seem that our daughter's illness was typhoid fever. We loaded her into the car and took her back to Baltimore, where her doctor put her on drugs and prescribed a long bed-rest. She lay in bed six days, looking wretched and calling for fluids and cold cloths. On the seventh day she got up her same old healthy self, and the illness was declared to be not typhoid fever after all but a simple virus, and we shipped her back to Virginia on the evening train. The next day I was free to start writing again but sat, instead, on the couch in my study, staring blankly at the wall.

I could draw some conclusions here about the effect that being a woman/wife/mother has upon my writing, except that I am married to a writer who is also a man/husband/father. He published his first novel while he was a medical student in Iran; then he came to America to finish his training. His writing fell by the wayside, for a long while. You can't be on call in the emergency room for twenty hours and write a novel during the other four. Now he's a child psychiatrist, full-time, and he writes his novels in the odd moments here and there—when he's not preparing a lecture, when he's not on the phone with a patient, when he's not attending classes at the psychoanalytic institute. He writes in Persian, still, in those black-and-white speckled composition books. Sometimes one of the children will interrupt him in English and he will answer in Persian, and they'll say, "What?" and he'll look up blankly, and it seems a sheet has to fall from in front of his eyes before he remembers where he is and switches to English. Often, I wonder what he would be doing now if he didn't have a family to support. He cares deeply about his writing and he's very good at it, but every morning at five-thirty he gets up and puts on a suit and tie and drives in the dark to the hospital. Both of us, in different ways, seem to be hewing our creative time in small, hard chips from our living time.

Occasionally, I take a day off. I go to a friend's house for lunch, or weed the garden, or rearrange the linen closet. I notice that at the end of one of these days, when my husband asks me what I've been doing, I tend to exaggerate any hardships I may have encountered. ("A pickup nearly sideswiped me on Greenspring Avenue. I stood in line an hour just trying to buy the children some flip-flops.") It seems sinful to have lounged around so. Also, it seems sinful that I have more choice than my husband as to whether or not to undertake any given piece of work. I can refuse to do an article if it doesn't appeal to me, refuse to change a short story, refuse to hurry a book any faster than it wants to go—all luxuries. My husband, on the other hand, is forced to rise and go off to that hospital every blessed weekday of his life. *His* luxury is that no one expects him to drop all else for two weeks when a child has chicken pox. The only person who has no luxuries at all, it seems to me, is the woman writer who is the sole support of her children. I often think about how she must manage. I think that if I were in that position, I'd have to find a job involving manual labor. I have spent so long erecting partitions around the part of me that writes—learning how to close the door on it when ordinary life intervenes, how to close the door on ordinary life when it's time to start writing again—that I'm not sure I could fit the two parts of me back together now.

Before we had children I worked in a library. It was a boring job, but I tend to like doing boring things. I would sit on a stool alphabetizing Russian catalogue cards and listening to the other librarians talking around me. It made me think of my adolescence, which was spent listening to the tobacco stringers while I handed tobacco. At night I'd go home from the library and write. I never wrote what the librarians said, exactly, but having those voices in my ears all day helped me summon up my own characters' voices. Then our first baby came along—an insomniac. I quit work and stayed home all day with her and walked her all night. Even if I had found the time to write, I wouldn't have had the insides. I felt drained; too much care and feeling were being drawn out of me. And the only voices I heard now were by appointment—people who came to dinner, or invited us to dinner, and who therefore felt they had to make deliberate conversation. That's one thing writers never have, and I still miss it: the easy-going, on-again-off-again, gossipy murmurs of people working alongside each other all day.

I enjoyed tending infants (though I've much preferred the later ages), but it was hard to be solely, continually in their company and not to be able to write. And I couldn't think of any alternative. I know it must be possible to have a child raised beautifully by a housekeeper, but every such child I've run into has seemed dulled and doesn't use words well. So I figured I'd better stick it out. As it happened, it wasn't that long—five years,

from the time our first daughter was born till our second started
nursery school and left me with my mornings free. But while I
was going through it I thought it would be a lot longer. I couldn't
imagine any end to it. I felt that everything I wanted to write was
somehow coagulating in my veins and making me fidgety and
slow. Then after a while I didn't have anything to write anyhow,
but I still had the fidgets. I felt useless, no matter how many
diapers I washed or strollers I pushed. The only way I could
explain my life to myself was to imagine that I was living in a
very small commune. I had spent my childhood in a commune,
or what would nowadays be called a commune, and I was used
to the idea of division of labor. What we had here, I told myself,
was a perfectly sensible arrangement: one member was the
liaison with the outside world, bringing in money; another was
the caretaker, reading the Little Bear books to the children and
repairing the electrical switches. This second member might
have less physical freedom, but she had much more freedom to
arrange her own work schedule. I must have sat down a dozen
times a week and very carefully, consciously thought it all
through. Often, I was merely trying to convince myself that I
really did pull my own weight.

   This Iranian cousin who just had the baby: she sits home now
and cries a lot. She was working on her master's degree and is
used to being out in the world more. "Never mind," I tell her,
"you'll soon be out again. This stage doesn't last long."

   "How long?" she asks.

   "Oh ... three years, if you just have the one."

   "Three years!"

   I can see she's appalled. Her baby is beautiful, very dark and
Persian; and what's more, he sleeps—something I've rarely seen
a baby do. What I'm trying to say to her (but of course, she'll
agree without really hearing me) is that he's worth it. It seems to
me that since I've had children, I've grown richer and deeper.
They may have slowed down my writing for a while, but when I
did write, I had more of a self to speak from. After all, who else in
the world do you *have* to love, no matter what? Who else can
you absolutely not give up on? My life seems more intricate. Also
more dangerous.

After the children started school, I put up the partitions in my mind. I would rush around in the morning braiding their hair, packing their lunches; then the second they were gone I would grow quiet and climb the stairs to my study. Sometimes a child would come home early and I would feel a little tug between the two parts of me; I'd be absent-minded and short-tempered. Then gradually I learned to make the transition more easily. It feels like a sort of string that I tell myself to loosen. When the children come home, I drop the string and close the study door and that's the end of it. It doesn't always work perfectly, of course. There are times when it doesn't work at all: if a child is sick, for instance, I can't possibly drop the children's end of the string, and I've learned not to try. It's easier just to stop writing for a while. Or if they're home but otherwise occupied, I no longer attempt to sneak off to my study to finish that one last page; I know that instantly, as if by magic, assorted little people will be pounding on my door requiring Band-Aids, tetanus shots, and a complete summation of the facts of life.

Last spring, I bought a midget tape recorder to make notes on. I'd noticed that my best ideas came while I was running the vacuum cleaner, but I was always losing them. I thought this little recorder would help. I carried it around in my shirt pocket. But I was ignoring the partitions, is what it was; I was letting one half of my life intrude upon the other. A child would be talking about her day at school and suddenly I'd whip out the tape recorder and tell it, "Get Morgan out of that cocktail party; he's not the type to drink." "Huh?" the child would say. Both halves began to seem ludicrous, unsynchronized. I took the recorder back to Radio Shack.

A few years ago, my parents went to the Gaza Strip to work for the American Friends Service Committee. It was a lifelong dream of my father's to do something with the AFSC as soon as all his children were grown, and he'd been actively preparing for it for years. But almost as soon as they got there, my mother fell ill with a mysterious fever that neither the Arab nor the Israeli hospitals could diagnose. My parents had to come home for her treatment, and since they'd sublet their house in North Carolina, they had to live with us. For four months, they stayed here—but only on a week-to-week basis, not knowing when they were going back, or whether they were going back at all, or how serious my mother's illness was. It was hard for her, of course, but it should have been especially hard in another way for my father, who had simply to hang in suspended animation for four months while my mother was whisked in and out of hospitals. However, I believe he was as pleased with life as he always is. He whistled Mozart and puttered around insulating our windows. He went on long walks collecting firewood. He strolled over to the meetinghouse and gave a talk on the plight of the Arab refugees. "Now that we seem to have a little time," he told my mother, "why not visit the boys?" and during one of her out-patient periods he took her on a gigantic cross-country trip to see all my brothers and any other relatives they happened upon. Then my mother decided she ought to go to a faith healer. (She wouldn't usually do such a thing, but she was desperate.) "Oh. Okay," my father said, and he took her to a faith healer, whistling all the way. And when the faith healer didn't work, my mother said, "I think this is psychosomatic. Let's go back to Gaza." My father said, "Okay," and reserved two seats on the next plane over. The children and I went to see them the following summer: my mother's fever was utterly gone, and my father drove us down the Strip, weaving a little Renault among the tents and camels, cheerfully whistling Mozart.

I hold this entire, rambling set of events in my head at all times, and remind myself of it almost daily. It seems to me that the way my father lives (infinitely adapting, and looking around him with a smile to say, "Oh! So *this* is where I am!") is also the way to slip gracefully through a choppy life of writing novels, plastering the dining room ceiling, and presiding at slumber parties. I have learned, bit by bit, to accept a school snow-closing as an unexpected holiday, an excuse to play seventeen rounds of Parcheesi instead of typing up a short story. When there's a midweek visitation of uncles from Iran (hordes of great, bald, yellow men calling for their glasses of tea, sleeping on guest beds, couches, two armchairs pushed together, and discarded crib mattresses), I have decided that I might as well listen to what they have to say, and work on my novel tomorrow instead.

I smile at the uncles out of a kind of clear, swept space inside me. What this takes, of course, is a sense of limitless time, but I'm getting that. My life is beginning to seem unusually long. And there's a danger to it: I could wind up as passive as a piece of wood on a wave. But I try to walk a middle line.

I was standing in the schoolyard waiting for a child when another mother came up to me. "Have you found work yet?" she asked. "Or are you still just writing?"

Now, how am I supposed to answer that?

I could take offense, come to think of it. Maybe the reason I didn't is that I halfway share her attitude. They're *paying* me for this? For just writing down untruthful stories? I'd better look around for more permanent employment. For I do consider writing to be a finite job. I expect that any day now, I will have said all I have to say; I'll have used up all my characters, and then I'll be free to get on with my real life. When I make a note of new ideas on index cards, I imagine I'm clearing out my head, and that soon it will be empty and spacious. I file the cards in a little blue box, and I can picture myself using the final card one day—ah! through at last—and throwing the blue box away. I'm like a dentist who continually fights tooth decay, working toward the time when he's conquered it altogether and done himself out of a job. But my head keeps loading up again; the little blue box stays crowded and messy. Even when I feel I have no ideas at all, and can't possibly start the next chapter, I have a sense of something still bottled in me, trying to get out.

People have always seemed funny and strange to me, and touching in unexpected ways. I can't shake off a sort of mist of irony that hangs over whatever I see. Probably that's what I'm trying to put across when I write; I may believe that I'm the one person who holds this view of things. And I'm always hurt when a reader says that I choose only bizarre or eccentric people to write about. It's not a matter of choice; it just seems to me that even the most ordinary person, in real life, will turn out to have something unusual at his center. I like to think that I might meet up with one of my past characters at the very next street corner. The odd thing is, sometimes I have. And if I were remotely religious, I'd believe that a little gathering of my characters would be waiting for me in heaven when I died. "*Then* what happened?" I'd ask them. "How have things worked out, since the last time I saw you?"

I think I was born with the impression that what happened in books was much more reasonable, and interesting, and *real*, in some ways, than what happened in life. I hated childhood, and spent it sitting behind a book waiting for adulthood to arrive. When I ran out of books I made up my own. At night, when I couldn't sleep, I made up stories in the dark. Most of my plots involved girls going west in covered wagons. I was truly furious that I'd been born too late to go west in a covered wagon.

I know a poet who says that in order to be a writer, you have to have had rheumatic fever in your childhood. I've never had rheumatic fever, but I believe that any kind of setting-apart situation will do as well. In my case, it was emerging from that commune—really an experimental Quaker community in the wilderness—and trying to fit into the outside world. I was eleven. I had never used a telephone and could strike a match on the soles of my bare feet. All the children in my new school looked very peculiar to me, and I certainly must have looked peculiar to them. I am still surprised, to this day, to find myself where I am. My life is so streamlined and full of modern conveniences. How did I get here? I have given up hope, by now, of ever losing my sense of distance; in fact, I seem to have come to cherish it. Neither I nor any of my brothers can stand being out among a crowd of people for any length of time at all.

I spent my adolescence planning to be an artist, not a writer. After all, books had to be about major events, and none had ever happened to me. All I knew were tobacco workers, stringing the leaves I handed them and talking up a storm. Then I found a book of Eudora Welty's short stories in the high school library. She was writing about Edna Earle, who was so slow-witted she could sit all day just pondering how the tail of the *C* got through the loop of the *L* on the Coca-Cola sign. Why, I knew Edna Earle. You mean you could *write* about such people? I have always meant to send Eudora Welty a thank-you note, but I imagine she would find it a little strange.

I wanted to go to Swarthmore College, but my parents

suggested Duke instead, where I had a full scholarship, because my three brothers were coming along right behind me and it was more important for boys to get a good education than for girls. That was the first and last time that my being female was ever a serious issue. I still don't think it was just, but I can't say it ruined my life. After all, Duke had Reynolds Price, who turned out to be the only person I ever knew who could actually teach writing. It all worked out, in the end.

I believe that for many writers, the hardest time is that dead spot after college (where they're wonder-children, made much of) and before their first published work. Luckily, I didn't notice that part; I was so vague about what I wanted to do that I could hardly chafe at not yet doing it. I went to graduate school in Russian studies; I scrubbed decks on a boat in Maine; I got a job ordering books from the Soviet Union. Writing was something that crept in around the edges. For a while I lived in New York, where I became addicted to riding any kind of train or subway, and while I rode I often felt I was nothing but an enormous eye, taking things in and turning them over and sorting them out. But who would I tell them to, once I'd sorted them? I have never had more than three or four close friends, at any period of my life; and anyway, I don't talk well. I am the kind of person who wakes up at four in the morning and suddenly thinks of what she should have said yesterday at lunch. For me, writing something down was the only road out.

You would think, since I waited so long and so hopefully for adulthood, that it would prove to be a disappointment. Actually, I figure it was worth the wait. I like everything about it but the paperwork—the income tax and protesting the Sears bill and renewing the Triple-A membership. I always did count on having a husband and children, and here they are. I'm surprised to find myself a writer but have fitted it in fairly well, I think. The only real trouble that writing has ever brought me is an occasional sense of being invaded by the outside world. Why do people imagine that writers, having chosen the most private of professions, should be any good at performing in public, or should have the slightest desire to tell their secrets to interviewers from ladies' magazines? I feel I am only holding myself together by being extremely firm and decisive about what I will do and what I will not do. I will write my books and raise the children. Anything else just fritters me away. I know this makes me seem narrow, but in fact, I *am* narrow. I like routine and rituals and I hate leaving home; I have a sense of digging my heels in. I refuse to drive on freeways. I dread our annual vacation. Yet I'm continually prepared for travel: it is physically impossible for me to buy any necessity without buying a travel-sized version as well. I have a little toilet kit, with soap and a nightgown, forever packed and ready to go. How do you explain that?

As the outside world grows less dependable, I keep buttressing my inside world, where people go on meaning well and surprising other people with little touches of grace. There are days when I sink into my novel like a pool and emerge feeling blank and bemused and used up. Then I drift over to the schoolyard, and there's this mother wondering if I'm doing anything halfway useful yet. Am I working? Have I found a job? No, I tell her.

I'm still just writing.

ALICE WALKER

ONE CHILD OF ONE'S OWN: A MEANINGFUL DIGRESSION WITHIN THE WORK(S)

SOMEONE asked me once whether I thought women artists should have children, and, since we were beyond discussing why this question is never asked artists who are men, I gave my answer promptly.

"Yes," I said, somewhat to my surprise. And, as if to amend my rashness, I added: "They should have children—*assuming this is of interest to them*—but only one."

"Why only one?" this Someone wanted to know.

"Because with one you can move," I said. "With more than one you're a sitting duck."

The year after my only child, R, was born, my mother offered me uncharacteristically bad advice: "You should have another one soon," said she, "so that R will have someone to play with, and so you can get it all over with faster."

Such advice does not come from what a woman recalls of her own experience. It comes from a pool of such misguidance women have collected over the millenia to help themselves feel less foolish for having more than one child. This pool is called, desperately, pitiably, "Women's Wisdom." In fact it should be called "Women's Folly."

The rebellious, generally pithy advice that comes from a woman's own experience more often resembles my mother's automatic response to any woman she meets who pines for

* In the work of this essay, and beyond this essay, I am indebted to the courageous and generous spirits of Tillie Olsen, Barbara Smith, and Gloria Steinem.—A.W.

children but has been serenely blessed with none: "If the Lord sets you free, be free indeed." *This crafty justification of both nonconformity and a shameless reveling in the resultant freedom is what women and slaves everywhere and in every age since the Old Testament have appropriated from the Bible.*

"No, thank you," I replied. "I will never have another child out of this body again."

"But why do you say that?" she asked breathlessly, perhaps stunned by my redundancy. "You married a man who's a wonderful fatherly type. He has so much love in him he should have fifty children running around his feet."

I saw myself stamping them out from around his feet like so many ants. If they're running around his feet for the two hours between the time he comes home from the office and the time we put them to bed, I thought, they'd be underneath my desk all day. Stamp, Stamp.

My mother continued: "Why," she said, "until my fifth child I was like a young girl. I could pick up and go anywhere I wanted to." She *was* a young girl. She was still under twenty-five when her fifth child was born, my age when I became pregnant with R. Besides, since I am the last child in a family of eight, this image of nimble flight is not the one lodged forever in my mind. I remember a woman struggling to get everyone else dressed for church on Sunday and only with the greatest effort being able to get ready on time herself. But, since I am not easily seduced by the charms of painful past experience, recalled in present tranquility, I did not bring this up.

At the time my mother could "pick up and go" with five children, she and my father traveled, usually, by wagon. I can see how that would have been pleasant: it is pleasant still in some countries—in parts of China, Cuba, Jamaica, Mexico, Greece, etc., etc. A couple of slow mules, ambling along a bright southern road, the smell of pine and honeysuckle, absence of smog, birds chirping. Those five dear little voices piping up in back of the wagon seat, healthy from natural foods: Plums! Bird! Tree! Flowers! Scuppernongs! Enchanting.

"The other reason I will never have another child out of this body is because having a child *hurts*, even more than toothache (and I am sure no one who has had toothache but not childbirth can imagine this), and it changes the body."

Well, there are several responses from the general supply of Women's Folly my mother could have chosen to answer this. She chose them all.

"*That* little pain," she scoffed. *(Although, from her own experience, which, caught in a moment of weakness for truth she has let slip, she has revealed that during my very own birth the pain was so severe she could not speak, not even to tell the midwife I had been born, and that because of the pain she was sure she would die—a thought that no doubt, under the circumstances, afforded relief. Instead, she blacked out, causing me to be almost smothered by the bedclothes.)* "That pain is over before you know it." That is response #1. #2 is, "The thing about that *kind* of pain is that it does a funny thing to a woman *(Uh-oh, I thought, this is going to be the Women's Folly companion to the 'women sure are funny creatures,' stuff)*; looks like the more it hurts you to give birth, the more you love the child." *(Is that why she loves me so much, I wonder. Naturally, I had wanted to be loved for myself not for her pain.)* #3. "Sometimes the pain, *they say*, isn't even real. Well, not as real as it feels at the time." *(This one deserves comment made only with blows, and is one of the reasons women sometimes experience muscle spasms around their mothers.)* And then, #4, the one that angers me most of all: "Another thing about the pain, *you soon forget it.*"

Am I mistaken in thinking I have never forgotten a pain in my life? Even those at parties, I remember.

"I remember every moment of it perfectly," I said. "Furthermore, I don't like stretch marks. I hate them, especially on my thighs" (which are otherwise gorgeous, and of which I am vain). Nobody had told me that my body, after bearing a child, would not be the same. I had heard things like: "Oh, your figure, and especially your breasts [of which I am also vain] will be better than ever." They sagged.

Well, why did I have a child in the first place?

Curiosity. Boredom. Avoiding the draft. Of these three reasons, I am redeemed only by the first. Curiosity is my natural state and

has led me headlong into every worthwhile experience (never
mind the others) I have ever had. It justifies itself. Boredom, in my
case, means a lull in my writing, emotional distance from
whatever political movement I am involved in, inability to
garden, read, or daydream—easily borne if there are at least a
dozen good movies around to attract me. Alas, in Jackson,
Mississippi, where my husband, M, and I were living in 1968,
there were few. About the draft we had three choices: the first,
C.O. status for M, was immediately denied us, as was "alterna
tive service to one's country," which meant, in his case,
legally desegregating a violent, frightening, rigidly segregated
Mississippi; the second was to move to Canada, which did not
thrill me, but which I would gladly have done rather than have M
go to prison. (Vietnam was never one of our choices.) The third
was, if M could not become twenty-six years old in time, to make
of him "a family man."

My bad days were spent in depression, anxiety, rage against the
war and a state of apprehension over the amount of rainfall there
is annually in Vancouver, and the slow rate of racial "progress" in
Mississippi. (Politicians were considered "progressive" if they
announced they were running for a certain office as candidates
"for *all* the people;" this was a subtle—they thought—
announcement to blacks that their existence was acknowledged.) I was also trying to become pregnant.

My good days were spent teaching, writing a simple history
pamphlet for use in black day-care centers in Jackson, recording
black women's autobiographies, making a quilt (African fabrics,
Mississippi string pattern), completing my second book, a novel,
and trying to become pregnant.

Three days after I finished the novel, R was born. The
pregnancy: the first three months I vomited. The middle three I
felt fine and flew off to look at ruins in Mexico. The last three I was
so huge—I looked like someone else, which did not please me.

What is true about giving birth is ... that it is miraculous. It
might even be the one genuine miracle in life (which is, by the
way, the basic belief of many "primitive" religions). The
"miracle" of nonbeing, death, certainly pales, I would think,
beside it. So to speak.

For one thing, though my stomach was huge and the baby (?!) constantly causing turbulence within it, I did not believe a baby, a person, would come out of me. I mean, look what had gone *in*. (Men have every right to be envious of the womb. I'm envious of it myself, and I have one.) But there she was, coming out, a black, curling lock of hair the first part to be seen, followed by nearly ten pounds of—a human being!

Reader, I *stared*.

But this hymn of praise I, anyhow, have heard before, and will not permit myself to repeat it, since there are, in fact, very few variations, and these have become boring and shopworn. They were boring and shopworn even at the birth of Christ, which is no doubt why "Virgin Birth" and "Immaculate Conception" were all the rage.

The point is, I was changed forever. From a woman whose "womb" had been, in a sense, her head; that is to say, certain small seeds had gone in, rather different if not larger or better "creations" had come out, to a woman who had "conceived" books in her head, and had also engendered at least one human being in her body.

Well, I wondered, with great fear, where is the split in me now? What is the damage? Was it true, as "anonymous"—so often a woman with distressing observations—warned: "Women have not created as fully as men because once she has a child a woman can not give herself to her work the way a man can ... etc, etc?" Was I, as a writer, *done for*? So much of Women's Folly, literary and otherwise, makes us feel constricted by experience rather than enlarged by it. Curled around my baby, feeling more anger and protectiveness than love, I thought of at least two sources of folly resistance Women's Folly lacks. It lacks all conviction that women have the ability to plan their lives for periods longer than nine months, and it lacks the courage to believe that experience, and the expression of that experience, may simply be different, *unique*, rather than "greater" or "lesser." The art or literature that saves our lives *is great to us*, in any case; more than that, as a Grace Paley character might say, we do not need to know.

I was, suddenly a mother. Combating the Women's Folly in my

own head was the first thing. The urge was primal: the desire to live and to appreciate my own unique life, as no one other than—myself.

It helped tremendously that by the time R was born I had no doubts about being a writer (doubts about making a *living* by writing, always). Write I did, night and day, *something*, and it was not even a choice, as having a baby was a choice, but a necessity. When I didn't write I thought of making bombs and throwing them. Of shooting racists. Of doing away—as painlessly and neatly as possible (except when I indulged in kamikaze tactics of rebellion in my daydreams) with myself. Writing saved me from the sin and *inconvenience* of violence—as it saves most writers who live in "interesting" oppressive times and are not afflicted by personal immunity.

I began to see, during a period when R and I were both ill—we had moved to Cambridge for a year and a half because I needed a change from Mississippi—that her birth, and the difficulties it provided us, joined me to a body of experience and a depth of commitment to my own life, hard to comprehend, otherwise. Her birth was the incomparable gift of seeing the world at quite a different angle than before, and judging it by standards that would apply far beyond my natural life. It also forced me to understand, viscerally, women's need for a store of Women's Folly and yet feel on firm ground in my rejection of it. But rejection also has its pain.

Distance is required, even now.

OF A GHASTLY YET USEFUL JOINT ILLNESS, WHICH TEACHETH OUR PILGRIM THAT HER CHILD MIGHT BE CALLED IN THIS WORLD OF TROUBLE THE LEAST OF HER MYRIAD OBSTACLES

Illness has always been of enormous benfit to me. It might even be said that I have learned little from anything that did not in some way make me sick.

The picture is not an unusual One: A mother and small child, new to the harshness of the New England winter in one of the worst flu waves of the century. The mother, flat on her back with flu, the child, burning with fever. The mother calls a name someone has given her, a famous pediatrician who writes for one of the largest of the women's magazines—in which he reveals himself to be sympathetic, witty, something of a feminist, even—to be told curtly that she should not call him at his home at any hour. Furthermore, he does not make house calls of any kind, and all of this is delivered in the coldest possible tone.

Still, since he is the only pediatrician she knows of in this weird place, she drags herself up next morning, when temperatures are below zero and a strong wind is blasting off the local river, and takes the child to see him. He is scarcely less chilly in person, but, seeing she is black, makes a couple of liberal comments to put her at her ease. She hates it when his white fingers touch her child.

A not unusual story. But it places mother and child forever on whichever side of society is opposite this man. She, the mother, begins to comprehend on deeper levels a story she has written years before she had a child, of a black mother, very poor, who, worried to distraction that her child is dying and no doctor will come to save him, turns to an old folk remedy for his illness, "strong horse tea." Which is to say, horse urine. The child dies, of course.

Now too the mother begins to see new levels in the stories she is at that moment—dizzy with fever—constructing. Why, she says, slapping her forehead, all history is current; all injustice continues on some level, somewhere in the world. "Progress" affects few. Only revolution can affect many.

It was during this same period when, risen from her bed of pain, her child well again and adapting to the cold, that the mother understood that her child, a victim of society as much as she herself—and more of one because as yet she was unable to cross the street without a guiding hand—was in fact the very least of her obstacles in her chosen work. This was brought home to her by the following experience, which, sickening as it was, yet produced in her several desired and ultimately healthful results—one of which was the easy ability to dismiss all people who thought and wrote as if she, herself, did not exist. By "herself" she of course meant multitudes, of which she was at any given time in history, a mere representative.

Our young mother had designed a course in black women writers which she proceeded to teach at an upper-class, largely

white, women's college (her students were racially mixed).
There she shared an office with a white woman feminist scholar
who taught poetry and literature. This woman thought black
literature consisted predominantly of Nikki Giovanni, whom she
had, apparently, once seen inadvertently on tv. Our young
mother was appalled. She made a habit of leaving books by
Gwendolyn Brooks, Margaret Walker, Toni Morrison, Nella
Larson, Paule Marshall, and Zora Neale Hurston face up on her
own desk, which was just behind the white feminist scholar's.
For the truly scholarly feminist, she thought, subtlety is enough.
She had heard that this scholar was writing a massive study of
women's imagination throughout the centuries, and what
women's imaginations were better than those displayed on her
desk, Our Mother wondered, what woman's imagination better
than her own, for that matter; but she was modest, and as I have
said, trusted to subtlety.

Time passed. The scholarly tome was published. Dozens of
imaginative women paraded across its pages. They were all
white. Papers of the status quo, like the *Times*, and liberal
inquirers like the *New York Review of Books* and the *Village
Voice*, and even feminist magazines such as *Ms.* (for which our
young mother was later to work) actually reviewed this work
with various degrees of seriousness. Yet to our young mother,
the index alone was sufficient proof that the work could not be
really serious scholarship, only serious white female chauvinism.
And for this she had little time and less patience.

In the prologue to her book The Female Imagination, *Patricia
Meyer Spacks attempts to explain why her book deals solely
with women in the "Anglo-American literary tradition." She
means, of course,* white *women in the Anglo-American tradition. Speaking of the books she has chosen to study, she writes:
"Almost all delineate the lives of white, middle-class women.
Phyllis Chesler has remarked, 'I have no theory to offer of Third
World female psychology in America. As a white woman, I'm
reluctant and unable to construct theories about experiences I
haven't had.' So am I: the books I talk about describe familiar
experience, belong to a familiar cultural setting; their particular immediacy depends partly on these facts. My bibliography*

balances works everyone knows (Jane Eyre, Middlemarch) *with works that should be better known* (The Story of Mary MacLane). *Still, the question remains: Why only these?"*

Why only these? Because they are white, and middle class, and because to Spacks, female imagination is only that—a limitation that even white women must find restrictive. Perhaps, however, this is the white female imagination, one that is "reluctant and unable *to construct theories about experiences I haven't had." Yet Spacks never lived in nineteenth-century Yorkshire, so why theorize about the Brontës?*

It took viewing The Dinner Party, *a feminist statement in art by Judy Chicago, to illuminate—as art always will—the problem. In 1973* when her book Through the Flower *was published, I was astonished, after reading it, to realize she knew nothing of black women painters. Not even that they exist. I was gratified therefore to learn that in* The Dinner Party *there was a place "set," as it were, for black women. The illumination came when I stood in front of it.*

All the other plates are creatively imagined vaginas (even the one that looks like a piano and the one that bears a striking resemblance to a head of lettuce: and of course the museum guide flutters about talking of "butterflies"!). The Sojourner Truth plate is the only one in the collection that shows—instead of a vaginal—a face. In fact, three faces. One, weeping (a truly clichéd tear), which "personifies" the black woman's "oppression," and another, screaming (a no less clichéd scream) with little ugly pointed teeth, "her heroism," and a third, in gimcracky "African" design, smiling; as if the African woman, pre-American slavery, or even today, had no woes. (There is of course a case to be made for being "personified" by a face rather than by a vagina, but that is not what this show is about.)

It occurred to me that perhaps white women feminists, no less than white women generally, cannot imagine black women have vaginas. Or if they can, where imagination leads them is too far to go.

However, to think of black women as women is impossible if you cannot imagine them with vaginas. Sojourner Truth

*certainly had a vagina, as note her lament about her children,
born of her body, but sold into slavery. Note her comment
(straightforward, not bathetic) that "when she cried out with a
mother's grief none but Jesus" heard her. Surely a vagina has to
be acknowledged when one reads these words. (A vagina the
color of raspberries and blackberries—or scuppernongs and
muscadines—and of that strong, silvery sweetness, with as well
a sharp flavor of salt).*

And through that vagina, children.

*Perhaps it is the black woman's children, whom the white
woman—having more to offer her own children, and certainly
not having to offer them slavery or a slave heritage or poverty
or hatred, generally speaking: segregated schools, slum neigh-
borhoods, the worst of everything—resents. For they must
always make her feel guilty. She fears knowing that black
women want the best for their children just as she does. But she
also knows black children are to have less in this world so that
her children, white children, will have more. (In some
countries, all.)*

*Better then to deny that the black woman has a vagina. Is
capable of motherhood. Is a woman.*

So, Our Mother* thought, cradling her baby with one hand,
while grading student papers with the other (she found teaching
extremely compatible with child care) the forces of the Opposition are in focus. Fortunately, she had not once believed that all
white women who called themselves feminists were any the less
racist, because work after ambitious work issued from the
country's presses, and, with but a few shining examples (and
Our Mother considered Tillie Olsen's *Silences* the *most* shining)
white women feminists revealed themselves as incapable as
white and black men of comprehending blackness and feminism
in the same body, not to mention within the same imagination.
By the time Ellen Moers's book on great *Literary Women* was
published in 1976—with Lorraine Hansberry used as a token of

---

* *I am indebted to the African writer Ama Ata Aidoo for my sense of the
usefulness of the phrase "Our Mother," after reading sections of her novel,
then in progress,* Our Sister Killjoy, or Reflections from a Black-eyed Squint.

what was not to be included, even in the future, in women's literature—Our Mother was well again. Exchanges like the following, which occurred wherever she was invited to lecture, she handled with aplomb:

White student feminist: "Do you think black women artists should work in the black community?"

Our Mother: "At least for a period in their lives. Perhaps a couple of years, just to give back some of what has been received."

White student feminist: "But if you say that black women should work in the black community, you are saying that race comes before sex. What about black *feminists*? Should *they* be expected to work in the black community? And if so, isn't this a betrayal of their feminism? Shouldn't they work with women?"

Our Mother: "But of course black people come in both sexes."

(Pause, while largely white audience, with sprinkle of perplexed blacks, ponders this possibility.)*

---

* *(In the preface to Ellen Moers's book* Literary Women: The Great Writers, *she writes: "Just as we are now trying to make sense of women's literature in the great feminist decade of the 1790s, when Mary Wollstonecraft blazed and died, and when, also Mme de Stael came to England and Jane Austen came of age, so the historians of the future will try to order women's literature of the 1960s and 1970s. They will have to consider Sylvia Plath as a woman writer and as a poet; but what will they make of her contemporary compatriot, the playwright Lorraine Hansberry? Born two years before Plath, and dead two years after her in her early thirties, Hansberry was not a suicide but a victim of cancer; she eloquently affirmed life, as Plath brilliantly wooed death.* Historians of the future will undoubtedly be satisfied with the title of Lorraine Hansberry's posthumous volume (named not by Hansberry, but by her former husband who became executor of her estate), To Be Young, Gifted and Black; and they will talk of her admiration for Thomas Wolfe; but of Sylvia Plath they will have to say "young, gifted, *and a woman.*" [Italics mine].*

It is, apparently, inconvenient, if not downright mind straining, for white women scholars to think of black women as women, perhaps because "woman" (like "man" among white males) is a name they are claiming for themselves, and themselves alone. Racism decrees that if they are now women (years ago they were ladies, but fashions change) then black women must, perforce, be something else. (While they were "ladies" black women could be "women," and so on.)

In any case, Moers expects "historians of the future" to be as dense as those in the past, and at least as white. It does not occur to her that they might be white women with a revolutionary rather than a reactionary or liberal approach to literature, let alone black women. Yet many are bound to be. Those future historians, working-class black and white women, should have no difficulty comprehending: "Lorraine Hansberry: Young, Gifted, Black,

OF OUR MOTHER'S CONTINUED PILGRIMAGE TOWARD TRUTH AT THE EXPENSE OF
VAIN PRIDE, OR: ONE MORE RIVER TO CROSS

*It was a river she did not even know was there. Hence her
difficulty in crossing it.*

Our Mother was glad, during the period of the above
revelations—all eventually salutary to her mental health—to
have occasion to address a large group of educated and successful black women. She had adequate respect for both education
and success, since both were often needed, she thought, to
comprehend the pains and anxieties of women who have
neither. She spoke praisingly of Black Herstory, she spoke as she
often did, deliberately of her mother (formerly missing from
both literature and history); she spoke of the alarming rise in the
suicide of young black women all over America. She asked that
these black women address themselves to this crisis. Adddress
themselves, in effect, to themselves.

Our Mother was halted in mid-speech. She was told she made
too much of Black Herstory. That she should not assume her
mother represented poor mothers all over the world (which she
did assume) and, furthermore, she was told, those to address
were black men; that, though it appeared more black women
than men were committing suicide, still everyone knew black
women to be the stronger of these two. Those women who
committed suicide were merely sick, apparently with an imagi-
nary or in any case a causeless disease. Furthermore, Our Mother
was told, "Our men must be supported in every way, *whatever
they do*." Since so many of "our men" were doing little at the
time but denigrating black women (and especially such
educated and "successful" black women as those assembled)
when they deigned to recognize them at all, and since this
denigration and abandonment was a direct cause of at least some
of the suicides, Our Mother was alarmed. Our Mother was
furious. Our Mother burst into tears (which some around her
thought a really strong black woman would not do).

*Activist, Woman, Eloquent Affirmer of Life," and: "Sylvia Plath: Young,
Gifted, White, Non-Activist Woman (in fact, fatally self-centered), Brilliant
Wooer of Death."*

However, Our Mother did not for one moment consider becoming something other than black and female. She was in the condition of twin "afflictions" for life. And, to tell the truth, she rather enjoyed being more difficult things in one lifetime than anybody else. She even regretted (at times) not being still desperately poor. She regretted (at times) her private sexual behavior was so much her own business it was in no sense provocative. She was, in her own obstacle-crazed way, a snob.

But it was while recuperating from this blow to her complete trust in *all* black women (which was foolish, as all categorical trust is, of course) that she began to understand a simple principle. People do not wish to appear foolish; to avoid the appearance of foolishness, they were willing to remain actually fools. This led directly to a clearer grasp of many black women's attitudes about the women's movement.

They had seen, perhaps earlier than she (she was notorious for her optimism regarding any progressive group effort) that white feminists are very often indistinguishable in their attitudes from any other white persons in America. She did not blame white *feminists* for the overturned buses of schoolchildren from Baton Rouge to Boston, as many black women did, or for the black schoolchildren beaten and spat upon. But look, just look, at the recent exhibit of women painters at the Brooklyn Museum!

("Are there no black women painters represented here?" one asked a white woman feminist.

"It's a women's exhibit!" she replied.)

OF THE NEED FOR INTERNATIONALISM, ALIGNMENT WITH NON-AMERICANS, NON-EUROPEANS, AND NON-CHAUVINISTS AND AGAINST MALE SUPREMACISTS OR WHITE SUPREMACISTS WHEREVER THEY EXIST ON THE GLOBE, WITH AN APPRECIATION OF ALL WHITE AMERICAN FEMINISTS WHO KNOW MORE OF NONWHITE WOMEN'S HERSTORY THAN "AND AIN'T I A WOMAN" BY SOJOURNER TRUTH

There was never a time when Our Mother thought, when someone spoke of "the women's movement," that this referred only to the women's movement in America. When she thought of women moving, she automatically thought of women all over the world. She recognized that to contemplate the American women's movement in isolation from the rest of the world would be—given the racism, sexism, elitism, and ignorance of so many American feminists—extremely defeating of solidarity among women as well as depressing to the most optimistic spirit. Our Mother had traveled and had every reason to understand that women's freedom was an idea whose time had come, an idea sweeping the world.

The women of China "hold up half the sky." They, who once had feet the size of pickles. The women of Cuba, fighting the combined oppression of African and Spanish macho, know that their revolution will be "shit" if they are the ones to do the laundry, dishes, and floors after working all day, side by side in factory and field with their men, "making the revolution." The women of Angola, Mozambique, and Eritrea have picked up the gun and propped against it demand their right to fight the enemy within as the enemy without their countries. The enemy within is the patriarchal system that has kept women virtual slaves throughout memory.

Our Mother understood that in America, white women who are truly feminist (for whom racism is inherently an impossibility, as long as some black people can also be conceived of as women) are largely outnumbered by *average* American white women for whom racism, inasmuch as it assures white privilege, is an accepted way of life. Naturally, many of these women, to be trendy, will leap to the feminist banner because it is now the place to be seen. What was required of women of color, many of whom have, over the centuries, and with the best of reasons, become racialists if not racists themselves, was to learn to distinguish between who was the real feminist and who was not, and to exert energy in feminist collaborations only when there is little risk of wasting it. The rigors of this discernment will invariably keep throwing women of color back upon themselves, where there is, indeed, so much work, of a feminist nature, to be done. From the stamping out of clitoridectomy and "female circumcision" in large parts of Arabia and Africa, to the heating of freezing urban tenements in which poor mothers and children are trapped alone to freeze to death. From the encouragement of women artists in Latin America to the founding of feminist publications for women of color in North America. From the stopping of pornography, child slavery, and forced prostitution and molestation of minors in the home and in Times Square, to the defense of women beaten and raped each Saturday night the world over by their husbands.

To the extent that black women disassociate themselves from the women's movement, they abandon their responsibilities to women throughout the world. This is a serious abdication from and misuse of radical black herstorical tradition: Harriet Tubman, Sojourner, Ida B. Wells, and Fannie Lou Hamer would not have liked it. Nor do I.

From my journal: Jackson, Mississippi, June 15, 1972:
R said today: "I can cook soup, and eggs, and windows!."
She also said, while drawing letters on the kitchen table: "A, D, and O." Then, "Oh-oh, the O is upside down!"

I feel very little guilt (most days) about the amount of time "taken from my daughter" by my work. I was amazed to discover I could read a book and she could exist at the same time. And how soon she learned that there are other things to enjoy besides myself. Between an abstracted, harassed adult and an affectionate sitter or neighbor's child who can be encouraged to return a ball, there is no contest, as one knows.

There *was* a day, when, finally after five years of writing *Meridian* (a book "about" the civil rights movement, feminism, socialism, the shakiness of revolutionaries and the radicalization of saints—the kind of book out of the political sixties that white feminist scholar Francine du Plessix Gray declared recently in the *New York Times Book Review* did not exist) I felt a pang.

I wrote this self-pitying poem:

> Now that the book is finished,
> now that I know my characters will live,
> I can love my child again.
> She need sit no longer
> at the back of my mind
> the lonely sucking of her thumb
> a giant stopper in my throat.

But this was as much celebration as anything. After all, the book *was* finished, the characters *would* live, and of course I'd loved my daughter all along. As for "the giant stopper in my throat," perhaps it is the fear of falling silent, *mute*, writers have from time to time. This fear is a hazard of the work itself, which requires a *severity* toward the self that is often over-whelming in its discomfort, more than it is the existence of one's child, who, anyway, by the age of seven, at the latest, is one's friend, and can be told of the fears one has, that she can, by listening to one, showing one a new dance step, perhaps, sharing a coloring book, or giving one a hug, help allay.

In any case, it is not my child who tells me I have no femaleness white women must affirm. Not my child who says I have no rights black men or black women must respect.

It is not my child who has purged my face from history and herstory and left mystory just that, a mystery; my child loves my face and would have it on every page, if she could, as I have loved my own parents' faces above all others, and have refused to let them be denied, or myself to let them go.

Not my child, who in a way *beyond* all this, but really of a piece with it, destroys the planet daily, and has begun on the universe.

We are together, my child and I. Mother and child, yes, but *sisters* really, against whatever denies us all that we are.

For a long time I had this sign, which I constructed myself, deliberately, out of false glitter, over my desk:

Dear Alice,

>   Virginia Woolf had madness;
>   George Eliot had ostracism,
>   somebody else's husband,
>   and did not dare to use
>   her own name.
>   Jane Austen had no privacy
>   and no love life.
>   The Brontë sisters never went anywhere
>   and died young
>   and dependent on their father.
>   Zora Hurston (ah!) had no money
>   and poor health.

You have R—who is
much more delightful
and less distracting
than any of the calamities
above.

BHARATI MUKHERJEE

A FOUR-HUNDRED-YEAR-OLD WOMAN

I was born into a class that did not live in its native language. I was born into a city that feared its future, and trained me for emigration. I attended a school run by Irish nuns, who regarded our walled-off school compound in Calcutta as a corner (forever green and tropical) of England. My "country"—called in Bengali *desh*, and suggesting more a homeland than a nation of which one is a citizen—I have never seen. It is the ancestral home of my father and is now in Bangladesh. Nevertheless, I speak his dialect of Bengali, and think of myself as "belonging" to Faridpur, the tiny green-gold village that was his birthplace. I was born into a religion that placed me, a Brahmin, at the top of its hierarchy while condemning me, as a woman, to a role of subservience. The larger political entity to which I gave my first allegiance—India—was not even a sovereign nation when I was born.

My horoscope, cast by a neighborhood astrologer when I was a week-old infant, predicted that I would be a writer, that I would win some prizes, that I would cross "the black waters" of oceans and make my home among aliens. Brought up in a culture that places its faith in horoscopes, it never occurred to me to doubt it. The astrologer meant to offer me a melancholy future; to be destined to leave India was to be banished from the sources of true culture. The nuns at school, on the other hand, insinuated that India had long outlived its glories, and that if we wanted to be educated, modern women and make something of our lives, we'd better hit the trail westward. All my girlhood, I straddled the seesaw of contradictions. *Bilayat*, meaning the scary, unknown "abroad," was both boom time and desperate loss.

I have found my way to the United States after many transit stops. The unglimpsed phantom Faridpur and the all too real Manhattan have merged as "desh." I am an American. I am an American writer, in the American mainstream, trying to extend it. This is a vitally important statement for me—I am not an Indian writer, not an exile, not an expatriate. I am an immigrant; my investment is in the American reality, not the Indian. I look on ghettoization—whether as a Bengali in India or as a hyphenated Indo-American in North America—as a temptation to be surmounted.

It took me ten painful years, from the early seventies to the early eighties, to overthrow the smothering tyranny of nostalgia. The remaining struggle for me is to make the American readership, meaning the editorial and publishing industries as well, acknowledge the same fact. (As the reception of such films as *Gandhi* and *A Passage to India* as well as *The Far Pavillions* and *The Jewel in the Crown* shows, nostalgia is a two-way street. Americans can feel nostalgic for a world they never knew.) The foreign-born, the exotically raised Third World immigrant with non-Western religions and non-European languages and appearance, can be as American as any steerage passenger from Ireland, Italy, or the Russian Pale. As I have written in another context (a review article in *The Nation* on books by Studs Terkel and Al Santoli), we are probably only a few years away from a Korean *What Makes Choon-li Run?* or a Hmong *Call It Sleep*. In other words, my literary agenda begins by acknowledging that America has transformed *me*. It does not end until I show how I (and the hundreds of thousands like me) have transformed America.

The agenda is simply stated, but in the long run revolutionary. Make the familiar exotic; the exotic familiar.

I have had to create an audience. I cannot rely on shorthand references to my community, my religion, my class, my region, or my old school tie. I've had to sensitize editors as well as readers to the richness of the lives I'm writing about. The most moving form of praise I receive from readers can be summed up in three words: *I never knew*. Meaning, I see these people (call them Indians, Filipinos, Koreans, Chinese) around me all the time and I never knew they had an inner life. I never knew they schemed and cheated, suffered, felt so strongly, cared so passionately. When even the forms of praise are so rudimentary, the writer knows she has an inexhaustible fictional population to enumerate. Perhaps even a mission, to appropriate a good colonial word.

I have been blessed with an enormity of material. I can be Chekhovian and Tolstoyan—with melancholy and philosophical perspectives on the breaking of hearts as well as the fall of civilizations—and I can be a brash and raucous homesteader, Huck Finn and Woman Warrior, on the unclaimed plains of American literature. My material, reduced to jacket-flap copy, is the rapid and dramatic transformation of the United States since the early 1970s. Within that perceived perimeter, however, I hope to wring surprises.

Yet (I am a writer much given to "yet") my imaginative home is also in the tales told by my mother and grandmother, the world of the Hindu epics. For all the hope and energy I have placed in the process of immigration and accommodation—I'm a person who couldn't ride a public bus when she first arrived, and now I'm someone who watches tractor pulls on obscure cable channels—there are parts of me that remain Indian, parts that slide against the masks of newer selves. The form that my stories and novels take inevitably reflects the resources of Indian mythology—shape-changing, miracles, godly perspectives. My characters can, I hope, transcend the straitjacket of simple psychologizing. The people I write about are culturally and politically several hundred years old: consider the history they have witnessed (colonialism, technology, education, liberation, civil war, uprooting). They have shed old identities, taken on new ones, and learned to hide the scars. They may sell you newspapers, or clean your offices at night.

Writers (especially American writers, weaned on the luxury of affluence and freedom) often disavow the notion of a "literary duty" or "political consciousness," citing the all-to-frequent examples of writers ruined by their shrill commitments. Glibness abounds on both sides of the argument, but finally I have to side with my "Third World" compatriots: I do have a duty, beyond telling a good story or drawing a convincing character. My duty is to give voice to continents, but also to redefine the nature of *American* and what makes an American. In the process, work like mine and dozens like it will open up the canon of American literature.

It has not been an easy transition, from graduate student to citizen, from natural-born expatriate to the hurly-burly of immigration. My husband (Clark Blaise) and I spent fifteen years in his *desh* of Canada, and Canada was a country that discouraged the very process of assimilation. Eventually, it also discouraged the very presence of "Pakis" in its midst, and in 1980, a low point in our lives, we left, gave up our tenured, full-professor lives for the free-lancing life in the United States.

We were living in Iowa City in 1983 when Emory University called me to be writer-in-residence for the winter semester. My name, apparently, had been suggested to them by an old friend. I hadn't published a book in six years (two earlier novels, *The Tiger's Daughter* and *Wife*, as well as our joint nonfiction study, *Days and Nights in Calcutta*, were out of print) but somehow Emory didn't hold it against me.

Atlanta turned out to be the luckiest writing break of my life. For one of those mysterious reasons, stories that had been gathering in me suddenly exploded. I wrote nearly all the stories in *Darkness* (Penguin, 1985) in those three months. I finally had a glimpse of my true material, and that is immigration. In other words, transformation—not preservation. I saw myself and my own experience refracted through a dozen separate lives. Clark, who remained in Iowa City until our younger son finished high school, sent me newspaper accounts, and I turned them into stories. Indian friends in Atlanta took me to dinners and table gossip became stories. Suddenly, I had begun appropriating the American language. My stories were about the hurly-burly of the unsettled magma between two worlds.

Eventually—inevitably—we made our way to New York. My next batch of stories (*The Middleman and Other Stories*, Grove, 1988) appropriate the American language in ways that are personally most satisfying to me (one Chicago reviewer likened it to Nabokov's *Lolita*), and my characters are now as likely to be

American as immigrant, and Chinese, Filipino, or Middle Eastern as much as Indian. That book has enjoyed widespread support both critically and commercially, and empowered me to write a new novel, *Jasmine*, and to contract for a major work, historical in nature, that nevertheless incorporates a much earlier version of my basic theme, due for completion in the next three years. *Days and Nights in Calcutta* is being made into a feature film.

My theme is the making of new Americans. Wherever I travel in the (very) Old World, I find "Americans" in the making, whether or not they ever make it to these shores. I see them as dreamers and conquerors, not afraid of transforming themselves, not afraid of abandoning some of their principles along the way. In *Jasmine*, my "American" is born in a Punjabi village, marries at fourteen, and is widowed at sixteen. Nevertheless, she is an American and will enter the book as an Iowa banker's wife.

Ancestral habits of mind can be constricting; they also confer one's individuality. I know I can appropriate the American language, but I can never be a minimalist. I have too many stories to tell. I am aware of myself as a four-hundred-year-old woman, born in the captivity of a colonial, pre-industrial oral culture and living now as a contemporary New Yorker.

My image of artistic structure and artistic excellence is the Moghul miniature painting with its crazy foreshortening of vanishing point, its insistence that everything happens simultaneously, bound only by shape and color. In the miniature paintings of India, there are a dozen separate foci, the most complicated stories can be rendered on a grain of rice, the corners are as elaborated as the centers. There is a sense of the interpenetration of all things. In the Moghul miniature of my life, there would be women investigating their bodies with mirrors, but they would be doing it on a distant balcony under fans wielded by bored serving girls; there would be a small girl listening to a bent old woman; there would be a white man eating popcorn and watching a baseball game; there would be cocktail parties and cornfields and a village set among rice paddies and skyscrapers. In a sense, I wrote that story, "Courtly Vision," at the end of *Darkness*. And in a dozen other ways I'm writing it today, and I will be writing, in the Moghul style, till I get it right.

TONI CADE BAMBARA

WHAT IT IS I THINK I'M DOING ANYHOW

WINTER 1979. We are now in the fourth year of the last quarter of the twentieth century. And the questions that face the millions of us on the earth are—in whose name will the twenty-first century be claimed? Can the planet be rescued from the psychopaths? Where are the evolved, poised-for-light adepts who will assume the task of administering power in a human interest, of redefining power as being not the privilege or class right to define, deform, and dominate but as the human responsibility to define, transform, and develop?

The previous quarter-century, from 1950 to 1975, was an era hallmarked by revolution, a period in which we experienced a radical shift in the political-power configurations of the globe. The current quarter, from 1976 to 2000, is also characterized by revolution, a period in which we are awakening to and experiencing a profound change in the psychic-power configurations of the globe.

There is a war going on and a transformation taking place. That war is not simply the contest between the socialist camp and the capitalist camp over which political/economic/social arrangement will enjoy hegemony in the world, nor is it simply the battle over turf and resources. Truth is one of the issues in this war. The truth, for example, about inherent human nature, about our potential, our agenda as earth people, our destiny.

Writing is one of the ways I participate in struggle—one of the ways I help to keep vibrant and resilient that vision that has kept the Family going on. Through writing I attempt to celebrate the tradition of resistance, attempt to tap Black potential, and try to join the chorus of voices that argues that exploitation and misery are neither inevitable nor necessary. Writing is one of the ways I participate in the transformation—one of the ways I practice the commitment to explore bodies of knowledge for the usable wisdoms they yield. In writing, I hope to encourage the fusion of those disciplines whose split (material science versus metaphysics versus aesthetics versus politics versus ...) predisposes us to accept fragmented truths and distortions as the whole. Writing is one of the ways I do my work in the world.

There are no career labels for that work, no facile terms to describe the tasks of it. Suffice to say that I do not take lightly the fact that I am on the earth at this particular time in human history, and am here as a member of a particular soul group and of a particular sex, having this particular adventure as a Pan-Africanist-socialist-feminist in the United States. I figure all that means something—about what I'm here to understand and to do.

Of all the mothers in the world I might have been born to, I was born at a particular moment to mine and to no other. As a kid with an enormous appetite for knowledge and a gift for imagining myself anywhere in the universe, I always seemed to be drawn to the library or to some music spot or to 125th Street and Seventh Avenue, Speaker's Corner, to listen to Garveyites, Father Diviners, Rastafarians, Muslims, trade unionists, communists, Pan-Africanists. And when I recall the host of teachers who have crossed my path and always right on time, so unfull of shit, so unlike the terrified and lost salaried teachers in the schools— and not only that, but having managed to survive Mather Academy boarding school's diet to come of age in the sixties— and all the while having some swamphag all up in my face asking me about my dreams (have I had a vision yet, have the voices given me instructions yet)—certainly it all means something. This is, after all, not a comic book. It's my life. So I pay attention. And I understand that I am being groomed to perform particular work in this world. Writing is one of the ways I try to do it.

The old folks say, "It's not how little we know that hurts so, but that so much of what we know ain't so." As a mother, teacher, writer, community worker, neighbor, I am concerned about accurate information, verifiable facts, sound analyses, responsible research, principled study, and people's assessment of the meaning of their lives. I'm interested in usable truths. Which means rising above my training, thinking better than I've been taught, developing a listening habit, making the self available to intelligence, engaging in demystification, and seeking out teachers at every turn. In many respects the writings are notebooks I'm submitting to those teachers for examination. There have been a host of teachers. Once I thought anyone with enthusiasm about information was a good teacher. Then, anyone with an analysis of this country who could help illuminate the condition, status, and process of the Family, who could help me decide how to put my wrath and my skills to the service of folks who sustain me. Later, anyone who could throw open the path and lead me back to the ancient wisdoms was teacher. In more recent times, any true dialectician (material/spiritual) who could increase my understanding of all, I say all, the forces afoot in the universe was teacher. I'm entering my forties with more simplistic criteria—anyone with a greater capacity for love than I is a valuable teacher. And when I look back on the body of book reviews I've produced in the past fifteen years, for all their socioideolitero brilliant somethinorother, the underlying standard always seemed to be—Does this author here genuinely love his/her community?

The greatest challenge in writing, then, in the earlier stages was to strike a balance between candor, honesty, integrity, and truth—terms that are fairly synonomous for crossword puzzlers and thesaurus ramblers but hard to equate as living actions. Speaking one's mind, after all, does not necessarily mean one is in touch with the truth or even with the facts. Being honest and frank in terms of my own where—where I'm at at a given point in my political/spiritual/etc. development—is not necessarily in my/our interest to utter, not necessarily in the interest of health, wholesomeness. Certain kinds of poisons, for example—rage, bitterness, revenge—don't need to be in the atmosphere, not to mention in my mouth. I don't, for example, hack up racists and stuff them in metaphorical boxes. I do not wish to lend them energy, for one thing. Though certainly there are "heavies" that people my stories. But I don't, for example, conjure up characters for the express purpose of despising them, of breaking their

humps in public. I used to be astounded at Henry James et al., so
nice nasty about it too, soooo refined. Gothic is of no interest to
me. I try not to lend energy to building grotesqueries, depicting
morbid relationships, dramatizing perversity. Folks come up to
me 'lowing as how since I am a writer I would certainly want to
hear blah, blah, blah, blah. They dump shit all over me, tell me
about every ugly overheard and lived-through nightmare ima-
ginable. They've got the wrong writer. The kid can't use it. I
straightaway refer them to the neighborhood healer, certain that
anyone so intoxicated would surely welcome a cleansing. But
they persist—"Hey, this is for real, square business. The truth." I
don't doubt that the horror tales are factual. I don't even doubt
that ugly is a truth for somebody ... somehow. But I'm not
convinced that ugly is *the* truth that can save us, redeem us. The
old folks teach that. Be triflin' and ugly and they say, "Deep
down, gal, you know that ain't right," appealing to a truth about
our deep-down nature. Good enough for me. Besides, I can't get
happy writing ugly weird. If I'm not laughing while I work, I
conclude that I am not communicating nourishment, since
laughter is the most sure-fire healant I know. I don't know all my
readers, but I know well for whom I write. And I want for them
no less than I want for myself—wholesomeness.

It all sounds so la-di-da and tra-la-la. I can afford to be sunny.
I'm but one voice in the chorus. The literature(s) of our time are
a collective effort, dependent on so many views, on so many
people's productions. I am frequently asked to name my favorite
writer, or the one writer who best captures the Black experience, or the one sister who is really doing it. What can I do but
crack up and stuff another carrot in the juicer? No way in the
world I can swing over to that frame of reference so dominated
by solo-voice thinking. Given the range of experiences available
to a soul having the human adventure in this time and place,
given that we have just begun to tap the limit-less reservoir of
cultural, societal, global, possibilities. Hell, there aren't even
phrases in the languages for half the things happening just on the
block where I live, not yet anyhow. Who could possibly be this
one writer that interviewers and reviewers are always harping
about? I read everybody I can get to, and I appreciate the way

"American literature" is being redefined now that the Black community is dialoguing without defensive postures, now that the Puerto Rican writers are coming through loud and clear, and the Chicano and Chicana writers, and Native American and Asian-American. ... There's a lot of work to do, a lot of records to get straight, a lot of living to share, a lot to plumb. This reader wants it all—the oddball, the satiric, the grim, the ludicrous, what have you. As for my own writing, I prefer the upbeat. It pleases me to blow three or four choruses of just sheer energetic fun and optimism, even in the teeth of rats, racists, repressive cops, bomb lovers, irresponsibles, murderers. I am convinced, I guess, that everything will be all right.

When I originally drafted the title story of my first story collection, *Gorilla, My Love*, the tone was severe, grim. The confrontations between the kid and the adults who so nonchalantly lie to and de-spirit little kids were raging red. Writing in a rage can produce some interesting pyrotechnics, but there are other ways to keep a fire ablaze, it seems to me. Besides, I know that everything will be O.K. for that little girl, so tough, so compassionate, so brave. Her encounter with the movie manager who put a come-on title on the marquee and then screened another movie altogether, and her encounter with her uncle who promised to marry her when she grew up and then turned right around and married some full-grown woman—those are rehearsals that will hold her in good stead in later encounters with more menacing and insidious people. That's second of all. first of all, while little kids' lives are most definitely characterized by intense anger over the injustices heaped upon them, it's not an anger that can sustain itself for twelve typewritten pages. Bunny rabbits and new socks and the neighbor kid's skates have a way of distracting kids. So clearly I had to solve a problem in pitch and voice. Once I could grin/cry through it, the writing felt right. Readers seem to laugh through it as well, as I've observed on subways, in laundromats, in libraries, and classrooms. And the lesson is not missed. So, as my classroom experience as a teacher has taught me, there are hipper ways to get to gut and brain than with hot pokers and pincers.

"Broken-field Running," in the 1977 collection *The Sea-birds*

Are Still Alive, was more of a challenge. It wasn't so much a problem in pitch as a problem in balancing the elements of mood. I'd been observing architectural changes in my community since the street rebellions. Schools, public housing, parks were being designed in such a way as to wreck community sovereignty, to render it impossible for neighbors to maintain surveillance and security of turf. I was enraged. I wrote a blazing essay on the subject, snarling, shooting from both hips. Hadn't a clue as to how to finish it or to whom to send it. Wrote a story instead. The first problem then was balancing the essay voice and the story voice; the second to keep the two dominant emotions of the narrator stabilized, in tension. The story is an odd sort of moody piece about a combatant, a teacher whose faith is slipping, whose belief in the capacity for transformation is splintering. I was trying to get at how difficult it is to maintain the fervent spirit at a time when the Movement is mute, when only a few enclaves exist. The teacher's work, her friend, her training, and most of all her responsibility to the children help to keep her centered, help to keep her in touch with the best of herself. But her task is rough.

Time out to say this—I often read in reviews that my stories are set in the sixties and are nostalgic and reminiscent of days when revolution was believed in. News to me. With the exception of "The Long Night," all the stories in *Seabirds* are in the "right now" time they were drafted. I suppose for too many people the idea that struggle is neither new nor over is hard to grasp, that there is a radical tradition as old as the H.M.S. *Jesus* or whatever that ship was that hauled over the first boatload. Some weeks ago, I read from my new work at a workshop of novels-in-progress. It was an excerpt about an elderly woman recalling the days when she worked for the Sleeping Car Porters and organized Ida B. Wells clubs in Harlem. Two out of three people at the reading assumed that the novel was set in the late sixties and that the woman was talking about the earlier sixties. Gives a person pause. Amnesia is a hellafying thing. The impulse to pronounce the Movement dead ain't no joke either.

Back to "Broken-field Running." It was spring 1974 and I'd just returned from a rally at which I heard that genocide was a fact in the Colored World, that the struggle was all over cause nobody cared anymore and blah, blah, blah, blah, accompanied by statistics and all the evangelical zeal of the brimstone tent belters. So in that woe-is-us mood, I began work on the story. And before I knew it, my character Lacy had picked it up and run off with it. Even while she was slipping in the snow and so in need of all kinds of support now that the thousands of combatants of a few years ago were/are no longer very visible, she managed to horse around enough to keep the story from getting depressing—depression being, to my mind, a form of collaboration. The kids in her orbit after all, are proof, mandate, motive to keep on keeping on. I guess then, that the message is—and I am a brazenly "message" writer, which seems to unsettle many reviewers—that in periods of high consciousness, one has to build the network and the foundation to sustain one through periods of high conflict and low consciousness. What goes around, comes around, as folks say.

Of course it is difficult to maintain the faith and keep working toward the new time if you've had no *experience* of it, not *seen* ordinary people actually transform selves and societies. That is the back-and-forth of the story "The Apprentice" in *Seabirds*. The young sister who narrates the story underestimates her own ability to fashion a revolutionary outlook, for she's not seen what my other character, the organizer Naomi, has seen. We, however, know that she will grow. She's got fine spirit for all her caterwauling. And we suspect too, I imagine, that whatever moved her into the circle of community workers and made her an apprentice in the first place will continue to operate, to inform her choices. And too, Naomi is kinda fun to hang out with. And that is the way many join ranks, after all, through an attraction to a given person. It's like the gospel song instructs, "You never know who's watching you," who's taking you as a model. I seem to recall that I invited Naomi onto the scene as a way of answering the grim reapers at that 1974 rally. If you're trying to recruit people to a particular kind of work, the recruiter has to stand for something attractive. I'd be willing to follow Naomi anywhere. She has heart to spare.

I got a lot of mixed reactions about the story "The Organizer's

Wife" in *Seabirds*. Feminist types didn't like the title; some said
they refused to read the story because the title was such a
putdown. Others liked the fact that Virginia, the lead character,
kicked the preacher's ass for more reasons than for turning her
husband in but, nonetheless, would have been happier had she
left town or died in childbirth, by way of my protesting the
system. Some letters and calls said I should have had Graham, the
organizer, die some gruesome death in that southern jail to
protest, etc. Kill Graham off and have Virginia go batty, or leave,
or die in childbirth? What kind of message would that have been?
How would I have explained that to my daughter? She's looking
forward to growing up as a responsible change agent. I'm well
aware that we are under siege, that the system kills, that the
terms of race and class war have not altered very much. But
death is not a truth that inspires, that pumps up the heart, that
mobilizes. It's defeatist to dwell always on the consequences of
risks. It's proracist to assume we can't take a chance. I am not
interested in collaborating with the program of the forces that
systematically underdevelop. So Graham lives and Virginia
wakes up.

"The Organizer's Wife," written in 1975 and set in 1975, is a
love story, layer after layer. Lovers and combatants are not
defeated. That is the message of that story, the theme of the
entire collection, the wisdom that gets me up in the morning,
honored to be here. It is a usable truth.

I'm reminded of a rip-roaring visit to a couple, friends of mine,
who invited me to dinner and began discussing Charles
Johnson's wonderful book *Faith and the Good Thing*. Leaning
across the table at each other, rattling dishes, knocking over the
candlestick, they proceeded to debate with brandished forks
whether or not the author's burning up of a baby on page such
and such was metaphorical infanticide. I love literary dinner
conversation, especially of the passionate kind. "It's a metaphor,
an act of language," yelled Larry, tugging on his omnipresent cap
lest he blow his wig. "I don't care about all such as that," Eleanor
hollered, hiking up her gown to climb onto the table to come at
him to make her point. "He burned up that baby." I thoroughly
enjoyed the meal and the passion. And I'm thoroughly in

Eleanor's camp if I understand her right. Words are to be taken seriously. I try to take seriously acts of language. Words set things in motion. I've seen them doing it. Words set up atmospheres, electrical fields, charges. I've felt them doing it. Words conjure. I try not to be careless about what I utter, write, sing. I'm careful about what I give voice to. To drive Virginia nuts or Graham to death is not a message I want to send to my heart, my lungs, my brain. My daughter. My readers. Or, to the Grahams and Virginias. But then I come from a particular tradition. I identify with the championship tradition.

Ali, in his autobiography, *I Am the Greatest*, defines a champion as one who takes the telling blow on the chin and hits the canvas hard, can't possibly rally, arms shot, energy spent, the very weight of the body too heavy a burden for the legs to raise, can't possibly get up. So you do. And you keep getting up. *The Awakening* by Kate Chopin is not my classic. *Their Eyes Were Watching God* by Zora Neale Hurston is. Sylvia Plath and the other obligatory writers on women's studies list—the writers who hawk despair, insanity, alienation, suicide, all in the name of protesting woman's oppression, are not my mentors. I was raised on stories of Harriet Tubman, Ida B. Wells, Paul Robeson, and my grandmother, Annie, whom folks in Atlanta still remember as an early Rosa Parks. So Virginia does not go batty and Graham does not die. Were I to do them in, my granny would no doubt visit me in the night to batter me gingerly about the head and shoulders with an ancestral bone pulled out of the Ethiopic Ocean called the Atlantic.

In the title story of *Seabirds*, I once again focus on resistance rather than despair and dramatize too, I think, the power of words, of utterances. The story is set in Southeast Asia aboard a boat transporting various people with various agenda to the city where the liberation forces, the royalist troops, and the foreign imperialists battle. The central characters are a little girl and her mother. Both are combatants. Both have been tortured. Both resist. When the mother closes her eyes and shivers, the girl fears she is remembering her torture and will begin to chant the words that enable her to come through her ordeal: "Nothing, I'll tell you nothing. You'll never break our spirits. We cannot be defeated." I weave the chant into a flashback scene in which her mother, reliving the experience, thrashes about on the floor while the girl attempts to work a bit of wood between her teeth. I weave it again into the current scene:

> The little girl continued brushing and smoothing her mother's hair, wondering if the gentleman in shoes could be relied upon if her mother bolted. If she herself didn't panic, she would demand he jump to aid the minute the first words were blurted out. "Nothing, I'll tell you nothing." It would take nimble timing, for often the upper folks would not touch the miserable shoeless. "You'll never break our spirits." But then the engine was shut off and her mother relaxed, looking over the side, her face full in the wind. "We cannot be defeated." So. It had been the vibrations of the boat, the little girl concluded, that had made her mother shiver. It had been the lurching of rough waters that had tipped the gentleman away from them.

I am currently working on a novel, though my druthers as writer, reader, and teacher is the short story. The short story makes a modest appeal for attention, slips up on your blind side and wrassles you to the mat before you know what's grabbed you. That appeals to my temperament. But of course it is not too shrewd to be exclusively a short story writer when the publishing industry, book reviewers, critics, and teachers of literature are all geared up for the novel. I gave myself an assignment based on an observation: there is a split between the spiritual, psychic, and political forces in my community. Not since the maroon experience of Toussaint's era have psychic technicians and spiritual folk (medicine people) and guerrillas (warriors) merged. It is a wasteful and dangerous split. The novel grew out of my attempt to fuse the seemingly separate frames of reference of the camps; it grew out of an interest in identifying bridges; it grew out of a compulsion to understand how the energies of this period will manifest themselves in the next decade.

I have three working titles to help me stay focused. "In the Last Quarter" is to remind myself of the period I'm "reading," to remind myself to script flashforwards as well as flashbacks, to remind myself that powerful events of the 1980s and 1990s (nuclear explosions, comet splashdowns, asteroid collisions) resonate in the present. Legionnaire's Disease, for example, may well be a backwash reverberation of the 1984 epidemics that many have predicted. The second title, "The Seven Sisters" (calling all numerologists, astrologists, astronomers, voodooists), helps me to stay within the law of As Above, So Below. In this case I'm trying to link the double helix of the Pleiades constellations (duplicated in the DNA molecule) with one of the central characters—a swamphag healer—and with a traveling troupe of seven women known as sisters of the yam, sisters of the plantain, sisters of the rice, sisters of the corn. These women from the ancient mother cultures perform multimedia shows at rallies and conferences and help me to argue the bridging of several camps: artists and activists, materialists and spiritualists, old and young, and of course the communities of color. The third working reminder is "The Salt Eaters." Salt is a partial antidote for snakebite. Bleeding the wound and applying the tourniquet, one also eats salt and applies a salt poultice to the wound. To struggle, to develop, one needs to master ways to neutralize poisons. "Salt" also keeps the parable of Lot's Wife to the fore. Without a belief in the capacity for transformation, one can become ossified. And what can we do with a saltlick in the middle of the projects, no cows there?

I'd never fully appreciated before the concern so many people express over women writers' work habits—how do you juggle the demands of motherhood, etc.? Do you find that friends, especially intimates, resent your need for privacy, etc.? Is it possible to wrench yourself away from active involvement for the lonely business of writing? Writing had never been so central an activity in my life before. Besides, a short story is fairly portable. I could narrate the basic outline while driving to the farmer's market, work out the dialogue while waiting for the airlines to answer the phone, draft a rough sketch of the central scene while overseeing my daughter's carrot cake, write the first version in the middle of the night, edit while the laundry takes a spin, and make copies while running off some rally flyers. But the novel has taken me out of action for frequent and lengthy periods. Other than readings and an occasional lecture, I seem unfit for any other kind of work. I cannot knock out a terse and pithy office memo any more. And my relationships, I'm sure, have suffered because I am so distracted, preoccupied, and distant. The short story is a piece of work. The novel is a way of life.

When I replay the tapes on file in my head, tapes of speeches I've given at writing conferences over the years, I invariably hear myself saying—"A writer, like any other cultural worker, like any other member of the community, ought to try to put her/his skills in the service of the community." Some years ago when I returned south, my picture in the paper prompted several neighbors to come visit. "You a writer? What all you write?" Before I could begin the catalogue, one old gent interrrupted with—"Ya know Miz Mary down the block? She need a writer to help her send off a letter to her grandson overseas." So I began a career as the neighborhood scribe—letters to relatives, snarling letters to the traffic chief about the promised stop sign, nasty letters to the utilities, angry letters to the principal about that confederate flag hanging in front of the school, contracts to transfer a truck from seller to buyer etc. While my efforts have been graciously appreciated in the form of sweet potato dumplings, herb teas, hair braiding, and the like, there is still much room for improvement—"For a writer, honey, you've got a mighty bad hand. Didn't they teach penmanship at that college?" Another example, I guess, of words setting things in motion. What goes around, comes around, as the elders say.

It will be a pleasure to get back to the shorts; they allow me to share. I much prefer to haul around story collections to prisons, schools, senior citizen centers, and rallies and then select from the "menu" something that suits the moment and is all of a piece. But the novel's pull is powerful. And since the breakthrough achieved in the sixties by the Neo-Black Arts Movement, the possibilities are stunning. Characters that have been waiting in the wings for generations, characters that did not fit into the roster of stereotypes, can now be brought down center stage. Now that I/we have located our audience, we are free to explore the limits of language. Now that American history, American literature, the American experience is being redefined by so many communities, the genre too will undergo changes. So I came to the novel with a sense that everything is possible. And I'm attempting to blueprint for myself the merger of these two camps: the political and the spiritual. The possibilities of healing that split are exciting. The implications of actually yoking those energies and of fusing that power quite take my breath away.

MAXINE HONG KINGSTON

THE COMING BOOK

W H E N a worker who knows how much more labor has to be done in no time nevertheless sits idle because caught in a situation where she can't work—visiting in a strange house over-night or eyes closed in the dentist's chair or darkness suddenly fallen deep in the woods—then the visions come assailing.

Once at the dentist's, I shut my eyes and saw The Book—a volume as thick as Joyce's *Ulysses* but not *Ulysses*—fly at me and fly past. Just before its appearance, I heard words from Joyce like music; not having read Joyce for years, I was surprised at the independence of memory. His words reeled out in entrancing rhythms flowing in small and large figure eights looping into infinity without periods and commas. The Joyce ended on the last Yes, and I heard No, no, no, no, and again No. I almost jumped out of the chair with elation. The universe had doubled! No, more than doubled; it was multiplying by millions. Joyce's day was but one day in a few people's lives, and there are millions of days more, millions of people more. A book of No would balance out a book of Yes, not cynically or unhappily but like a facing page. The Book had flown out of the distance and zoomed past my head.

I felt tired ahead of time for the work to be done to build The Book word by word. If I could finish it, I would never have to write again; in it would be the last word. So far we have only written approximations.

The Book begins with the sound of a telephone ringing, ringing, ringing. Also a radio is playing a rock song, hard electric rock words, which I've forgotten. If I write The Book, I'll have to invent that song.

That's all I glimpsed when The Book zipped by. I will have to make trails of words into that room to find out who answers the phone, who is calling, and what they talk about.

Right now I don't know who these people are or what the room looks like or what city it's in. But it is not me on the telephone, and not me who lives in that room. I wouldn't play a rock station that loud. So, with The Book, I will make a break from the "I" stories I have been writing.

"The telephone rang too loud again and again and again, crashed into the rock music, the top song on the top ten, at inflexible intervals. It was a warm afternoon. ..." There will next be a rushing about, turning down the radio, grabbing the phone before it stops ringing.

I can't follow this story any further. First I have to finish the stories I couldn't write during childhood because of the years it took to acquire vocabulary.

The Book's pace will be normal, no skips but one moment moving to the next like the phone's rings. No elisions like "As the years passed. ... I heard each full ring and the time before them. And each word of the song. The characters will rush about, but the narration will be deliberate—*ring ... ring ... ring*.

I did not *see* the radio or the telephone; The Book begins with two sounds, which are not proper "visions." But I am not an audile, and I believe that if I lose my sight, I will no longer be able to write. I like to look at poetry on the page, the spacing of the lines, the letters. I like rearranging by eye. Blindly composing by voice would bypass reason, miss precision. Both the sounds are modern sounds, technological noises, not the birds and rivers and winds that I like. Harsh rings. Harsh music. Not the epic symphonies that I hear (but can't remember because I don't know notation).

The second paragraph will begin the dialogue. The Book will be filled with voices as heard through machines. When read aloud, it will sound like the Twentieth Century. The reader will not need a visual imagination, only ears.

I heard somewhere that aural hallucinations are a more severe symptom of psychosis than visual ones. But in healthy people, auricular images may be only a more advanced form of imagination than pictures. (I also habitually hear what other people don't hear—firecrackers or gunshots, which may be Chinese music.) The Book will not be a collection of nonsense sounds but English words, a translation of music.

I told a woman who plays viola in a symphony orchestra how uncapturable music is, how I cannot think of organizing the music I hear, but only be its audience. But she said that writing is the most abstract form; the other forms have concomitant human sense organs; music has the ear, and painting the eye, sculpture the hands, and acting and dancing the voice and body. But writing, she said, does not have its organ. She began to cry; I'm not sure why.

I can feel the texture of The Book; it will be modern like science fiction, like black vinyl. The characters will not worry so much about food as they do in my present writings; they can afford phones and a sound system.

When alone, I am not aware of my race or my sex, both in need of social contexts for definition. Visions (and "aurisons"? "audisions"?) come to a human being alone; they are embarrassed away when people watch you humming to yourself or staring at nothing. Yet visions probably don't come from nowhere but grow from what we see everyday and live everyday, which is America. In America, Everyman—the universal human being—is white. (I have been watching a lot of television.) The Book may exclude me as first-person narrator, and the Chinese-American heroines who have interested me may disappear.

"Hello."

"Hello, is it you?"

"Yes. I mean No. Who is this?"

"It's me."

"Oh, it's you . What are you doing?"

"Nothing much. What about you?"

If The Book is an archetype, I needn't be the one to write it. Someone else can write what happens next, and I'd be happy to read it. You can have the opening if you want; it may save you a few moment's work.

You'd save me the time to examine some other sightings, like the town I saw when I got lost in the woods. Also, there were people calling, "We hear you. We're coming. This way. This way." The shingled roofs and white walls and windows turned out to be optical illusions made by the spaces between the leaves and the shaking leaves catching the sun. "This may be how I'll go," I said aloud. "I'll die of starvation and exposure lost in the mountains." When I'd circled the same landmarks twice, I sat on the ground and waited to get some ultimate message while facing death. The leaves and the insects kept on shimmering. Apparently you have no choice about what shows itself. What I did learn was: Don't trust deer trails; they meander and fade. Head downhill, where you'll come to a stream; follow it to town.

MARY GORDON

THE PARABLE OF THE CAVE OR:
IN PRAISE OF WATERCOLORS

ONCE, I was told a story by a famous writer. "I will tell you what women writers are like," he said. The year was 1971. The women's movement had made men nervous; it had made a lot of women write. "Women writers are like a female bear who goes into a cave to hibernate. The male bear shoves a pine cone up her ass, because he knows if she shits all winter, she'll stink up the cave. In the spring, the pressure of all that built-up shit makes her expel the pine cone, and she shits a winter's worth all over the walls of the cave."

That's what women writers are like, said the famous writer.

He told the story with such geniality; he looked as if he were giving me a wonderful gift. I felt I ought to smile; every one knows there's no bore like a feminist with no sense of humor. I did not write for two months after that. It was the only time in my life I have suffered from writer's block. I should not have smiled. But he was a famous writer and spoke with geniality. And in truth, I did not have the courage for clear rage. There is no seduction like that of being thought a good girl.

Theodore Roethke said that women poets were "stamping a tiny foot against God." I have been told by male but not by female critics that my work was "exquisite," "lovely," "like a watercolor." They, of course, were painting in oils. They were doing the important work. Watercolors are cheap and plentiful; oils are costly: their base must be bought. And the idea is that oil paintings will endure. But what will they endure against? fire? flood? Bombs? Earthquake? Their endurance is another illusion: one more foolish bet against nature, or against natural vulnerabilities, one more scheme, like fallout shelters, one more gesture of illusory safety.

There are people in the world who derive no small pleasure from the game of "major" and "minor." They think that no major work can be painted in watercolors. They think, too, that Hemingway writing about boys in the woods is major; Mansfield writing about girls in the house is minor. Exquisite, they will hasten to insist, but minor. These people join up with other bad specters, and I have to work to banish them. Let us pretend these specters are two men, two famous poets, saying, "Your experience is an embarrassment; your experience is insignificant."

I wanted to be a good girl, so I tried to find out whose experience was not embarrassing. The prototype for a writer who was not embarrassing was Henry James. And you see, the two specters said, proffering hope, he wrote about social relationships, but his distance gave them grandeur.

Distance, then, was what I was to strive for. Distance from the body, from the heart, but most of all, distance from the self as writer. I could never understand exactly what they meant or how to do it; it was like trying to follow the directions on a home permanent in 1959.

If Henry James had the refined experience, Conrad had the significant one. The important moral issues were his: men pitted against nature in moments of extremity. There are no important women in Conrad's novel, except for *Victory*, which, the critics tell us, is a romance and an exception. Despite the example of Conrad, it was all right for the young men I knew, according to my specters, to write about the hymens they had broken, the diner waitresses they had seduced. Those experiences were significant. But we were not to write about our broken hearts, about the married men we loved disastrously, about our mothers or our children. Men could write about their fears of dying by exposure in the forest; we could not write about our fears of being suffocated in the kitchen. Our desire to write about these experiences only revealed our shallowness; it was suggested we would, in time, get over it. And write about what? Perhaps we would stop writing.

And so, the specters whispered to me, if you want to write well, if you want us to take you seriously, you must be distant, you must be extreme.

I suppose the specters were not entirely wrong. Some of the literature that has been written since the inception of the women's movement is lacking in style and moral proportion. But so is the work of Mailer, Miller, Burroughs, Ginsberg. Their lack of style and proportion may be called offensive, but not embarrassing. They may be referred to as off the mark, but they will not be called trivial.

And above all I did not wish to be *trivial*; I did not wish to be embarrassing. But I did not want to write like Conrad, and I did not want to write like Henry James. The writers I wanted to imitate were all women: Charlotte Brontë, Woolf, Mansfield, Bowen, Lessing, Olsen. I discovered that what I loved in writing was not distance but radical closeness; not the violence of the bizarre but the complexity of the quotidian.

I lost my fear of being trivial, but not my fear of being an embarrassment. And so, I wrote my first novel in the third person. No one would publish it. Then a famous woman writer asked why I had written a first-person novel in the third person. She is a woman of abiding common sense, and so I blushed to tell her: "I wanted to sound serious. I didn't want to be embarrassing."

Only her wisdom made me write the novel I meant to. I can say it now: I will probably never read Conrad again; what he writes about simply does not interest me. Henry James I will love always, but it is not for his distance that I love him. The notion that style and detachment are necessary blood brothers is crude and bigoted. It is an intellectual embarrassment.

And I can say it now: I would rather own a Mary Cassatt watercolor than a Velasquez oil.

Here is the good side of being a woman writer: the company of other women writers, dead and living. My writer friends, all women, help me banish the dark specters. So does Katharine Mansfield; so does Christina Rossetti. I feel their closeness to the heart of things; I feel their aptness and their bravery.

I think it is lonelier to be a man writer than a woman writer now, because I do not think that men are as good at being friends to one another as women are. Perhaps, since they have not thought they needed each other's protection, as women have known we have needed each other's, they have not learned the knack of helpful, rich concern which centers on a friend's work. They may be worried, since they see themselves as hewers of wood and slayers of animals, about production, about the kind of achievement that sees its success only in terms of another's failure. They may not be as kind to one another; they may not know how. These are the specters that men now must banish. Our specters may be easier to chase. For the moment. They were not always so.

To this tale there should be an appendix, an explanation. Why was I so susceptible to the bad advice of men? What made me so ready to listen? Where did I acquire my genius for obedience?

I had a charming father. In many crucial ways, he was innocent of sexism, although he may have substituted narcissism in its place. He wanted me to be like him. He was a writer, an unsuccessful writer, and my mother worked as a secretary to support us. Nevertheless he was a writer; he could think of himself as nothing else. He wanted me to be a writer too. I may have been born to be one, which made things easier. He died when I was seven. But even in those years we had together I learned well that I was his child, not my mother's. His mind was exalted, my mother's common. That she could earn the money to support us was only proof of the ordinariness of her nature, an ordinariness to which I was in no way heir. So I was taught to read at three, taught French at six, and taught to despise the world of women, the domestic. I was a docile child. I brought my father great joy, and I learned the pleasures of being a good girl.

And I earned, as a good girl, no mean rewards. Our egos are born delicate. Bestowing pleasure upon a beloved father is much easier than discovering the joys of solitary achievements. It was easy for me to please my father; and this ease bred in me a desire to please men—desire for the rewards of a good girl. They are by no means inconsiderable: safety and approval, the warm, incomparable atmosphere created when one pleases a man who has vowed, in his turn, to keep the wolf from the door.

But who is the wolf?

He is strangers. He is the risk of one's own judgments, one's own work.

I have learned in time that I am at least as much my mother's daughter as my father's. Had I been only my mother's daughter it is very possible that I would never have written: I may not have had the confidence required to embark upon a career so valueless in the eyes of the commonsense world. I did what my father wanted; I became a writer. I grew used to giving him the credit. But now I see that I am the *kind* of writer I am because I am my mother's daughter. My father's tastes ran to the metaphysical. My mother taught me to listen to conversations at the dinner table; she taught me to remember jokes.

My subject as a writer has far more to do with family happiness than with the music of the spheres. I don't know what the nature of the universe is, but I have a good ear. What it hears best are daily rhythms, for that is what I value, what I would wish, as a writer to preserve.

My father would have thought this a stubborn predilection for the minor. My mother knows better.

MARGARET ATWOOD

NINE BEGINNINGS

1. *Why do you write?*

I've begun this piece nine times. I've junked each beginning.

I hate writing about my writing. I almost never do it. Why am I doing it now? Because I said I would. I got a letter. I wrote back *no*. Then I was at a party and the same person was there. It's harder to refuse in person. Saying *yes* had something to do with being nice, as women are taught to be, and something to do with being helpful, which we are also taught. Being helpful to women, giving a pint of blood. With not claiming the sacred prerogatives, the touch-me-not self-protectiveness of the artist, with not being selfish. With conciliation, with doing your bit, with appeasement. I was well brought up. I have trouble ignoring social obligations. Saying you'll write about your writing is a social obligation. It's not an obligation to the writing.

2. *Why do you write?*

I've junked each of nine beginnings. They seemed beside the point. Too assertive, too pedagogical, too frivolous or belligerent, too falsely wise. As if I had some special self-revelation that would encourage others, or some special knowledge to impart, some pithy saying that would act like a talisman for the driven, the obsessed. But I have no such talismans. If I did, I would not continue, myself, to be so driven and obsessed.

3. Why do you write?

I hate writing about my writing because I have nothing to say about it. I have nothing to say about it because I can't remember what goes on when I'm doing it. That time is like small pieces cut out of my brain. It's not time I myself have lived. I can remember the details of the rooms and places where I've written, the circumstances, the other things I did before and after, but not the process itself. Writing about writing requires self-consciousness; writing itself requires the abdication of it.

4. Why do you write?

There are a lot of things that can be said about what goes on around the edges of writing. Certain ideas you may have, certain motivations, grand designs that don't get carried out. I can talk about bad reviews, about sexist reactions to my writing, about making an idiot of myself on television shows. I can talk about books that failed, that never got finished, and about why they failed. The one that had too many characters, the one that had too many layers of time, red herrings that diverted me when what I really wanted to get at was something else, a certain corner of the visual world, a certain voice, an inarticulate landscape.

I can talk about the difficulties that women encounter as writers. For instance, if you're a woman writer, sometime, somewhere, you will be asked: *Do you think of yourself as a writer first, or as a woman first?* Look out. Whoever asks this hates and fears both writing and women.

Many of us, in my generation at least, ran into teachers or male writers or other defensive jerks who told us women could not really write because they couldn't be truck drivers or Marines and therefore didn't understand the seamier side of life, which included sex with women. We were told we wrote like housewives, or else we were treated like honorary men, as if to be a good writer was to suppress the female.

Such pronouncements used to be made as if they were the simple truth. Now they're questioned. Some things have changed for the better, but not all. There's a lack of self-confidence that gets instilled very early in many young girls, before writing is even seen as a possibility. You need a certain amount of nerve to be a writer, an almost physical nerve, the kind you need to walk a log across a river. The horse throws you and you get back on the horse. I learned to swim by being dropped into the water. You need to know you can sink, and survive it. Girls should be allowed to play in the mud. They should be released from the obligations of perfection. Some of your writing, at least, should be as evanescent as play.

A ratio of failures is built into the process of writing. The waste-basket has evolved for a reason. Think of it as the altar of the Muse Oblivion, to whom you sacrifice your botched first drafts, the tokens of your human imperfection. She is the tenth Muse, the one without whom none of the others can function. The gift she offers you is the freedom of the second chance. Or as many chances as you'll take.

5. Why do you write?

In the mid-eighties I began a sporadic journal. Today I went back through it, looking for something I could dig out and fob off as pertinent, instead of writing this piece about writing. But it was useless. There was nothing in it about the actual composition of anything I've written over the past six years. Instead there are exhortations to myself—to get up earlier, to walk more, to resist lures and distractions. *Drink more water*, I find. *Go to bed earlier*. There were lists of how many pages I'd written per day, how many I'd retyped, how many yet to go. Other than that, there was nothing but descriptions of rooms, accounts of what we'd cooked and/or eaten and with whom, letters written and received, notable sayings of children, birds and animals seen, the weather. What came up in the garden. Illnesses, my own and those of others. Deaths, births. Nothing about writing.

January 1, 1984. Blakeney, England. As of today, I have about 130 pp. of the novel done and its just beginning to take shape & reach the point at which I feel that it exists and can be finished and may be worth it. I work in the bedroom of the big

house, and here, in the sitting room, with the wood fire in the
fireplace and the coke fire in the dilapidated Raeburn in the
kitchen. As usual I'm too cold, which is better than being too
hot—today is grey, warm for the time of year, damp. If I got up
earlier maybe I would work more, but I might just spend more
time procrastinating—as now.

And so on.

6. Why do you write?

You learn to write by reading and writing, writing and reading.
As a craft it's acquired through the apprentice system, but you
choose your own teachers. Sometimes they're alive, sometimes
dead.

As a vocation, it involves the laying on of hands. You receive
your vocation and in your turn you must pass it on. Perhaps you
will do this only through your work, perhaps in other ways.
Either way, you're part of a community, the community of
writers, the community of storytellers that stretches back
through time to the beginning of human society.

As for the particular human society to which you yourself
belong—sometimes you'll feel you're speaking for it,
sometimes—when it's taken an unjust form—against it, or for
that other community, the community of the oppressed, the
exploited, the voiceless. Either way, the pressures on you will be
intense; in other countries, perhaps fatal. But even here—speak
"for women," or for any other group which is feeling the boot,
and there will be many at hand, both for and against, to tell you
to shut up, or to say what they want you to say, or to say it a
different way. Or to save them. The billboard awaits you, but if
you succumb to its temptations you'll end up two-dimensional.

Tell what is yours to tell. Let others tell what is theirs.

7. Why do you write?

Why are we so addicted to causality? *Why do* you *write?*
(Treatise by child psychologist, mapping your formative trau-
mas. Conversely: palm-reading, astrology and genetic studies,

pointing to the stars, fate, heredity.) *Why do you write?* (That is, why not do something useful instead?) If you were a doctor, you could tell some acceptable moral tale about how you put Band-Aids on your cats as a child, how you've always longed to cure suffering. No one can argue with that. But writing? What is it *for?*

Some possible answers: *Why does the sun shine? In the face of the absurdity of modern society, why do anything else? Because I'm a writer. Because I want to discover the patterns in the chaos of time. Because I must. Because someone has to bear witness. Why do you read?* (This last is tricky: maybe they don't.) *Because I wish to forge in the smithy of my soul the uncreated conscience of my race. Because I wish to make an axe to break the frozen sea within.* (These have been used, but they're good.)

If at a loss, perfect the shrug. Or say: *It's better than working in a bank.* Or say: *For fun.* If you say this, you won't be believed, or else you'll be dismissed as trivial. Either way, you'll have avoided the question.

8. *Why do you write?*

Not long ago, in the course of clearing some of the excess paper out of my workroom, I opened a filing cabinet drawer I hadn't looked into for years. In it was a bundle of loose sheets, folded, creased, and grubby, tied up with leftover string. It consisted of things I'd written in the late fifties, in high school and the early years of university. There were scrawled, inky poems, about snow, despair, and the Hungarian Revolution. There were short stories dealing with girls who'd had to get married, and dispirited, mousy-haired high-school English teachers—to end up as either was at that time my vision of Hell—typed finger-by-finger on an ancient machine that made all the letters half-red.

There I am, then, back in grade twelve, going through the writers' magazines after I'd finished my French Composition homework, typing out my lugubrious poems and my grit-filled stories. (I was big on grit. I had an eye for lawn-litter and dog turds on sidewalks. In these stories it was usually snowing

damply, or raining; at the very least there was slush. If it was
summer, the heat and humidity were always wiltingly high and
my characters had sweat marks under their arms; if it was spring,
wet clay stuck to their feet. Though some would say all this was
just normal Toronto weather.)

In the top right-hand corners of some of these, my hopeful
seventeen-year-old self had typed, "First North American Rights
Only." I was not sure what "First North American Rights" were; I
put it in because the writing magazines said you should. I was at
that time an aficionado of writing magazines, having no one else
to turn to for professional advice.

If I were an archeologist, digging through the layers of old
paper that mark the eras in my life as a writer, I'd have found,
at the lowest or Stone Age level—say around ages five to
seven—a few poems and stories, unremarkable precursors of
all my frenetic later scribbling. (Many children write at that
age, just as many children draw. The strange thing is that so
few of them go on to become writers or painters.) After that
there's a great blank. For eight years, I simply didn't write.
Then, suddenly, and with no missing links in between, there's
a wad of manuscripts. One week I wasn't a writer, the next I
was.

Who did I think I was, to be able to get away with this? What
did I think I was doing? How did I get that way? To these
questions I still have no answers.

9. Why do you write?

There's the blank page, and the thing that obsesses you. There's
the story that wants to take you over and there's your resistance
to it. There's your longing to get out of this, this servitude, to
play hooky, to do anything else: wash the laundry, see a movie.
There are words and their inertias, their biases, their insufficien-
cies, their glories. There are the risks you take and your loss of
nerve, and the help that comes when you're least expecting it.
There's the laborious revision, the scrawled-over, crumpled-up
pages that drift across the floor like spilled litter. There's the one
sentence you know you will save.

Next day there's the blank page. You give yourself up to it like a sleepwalker. Something goes on that you can't remember afterwards. You look at what you've done. It's hopeless.

You begin again. It never gets any easier.

ERICA JONG

BLOOD AND GUTS: THE TRICKY PROBLEM OF BEING A WOMAN WRITER IN THE LATE TWENTIETH CENTURY

T H E question of whether or not writers are affected by the politics of the times in which they live has always been a tricky one. Some part of them assuredly is—but whether it is the part that tunes into the communal unconscious and makes poems and novels is doubtful. Yet a writer is a person of his or her age and must live in it. For women writers the systematic discouragement even to *attempt* to become writers has been so constant and pervasive a force that we cannot consider their literary productions without somehow assessing the effects of that barrage of discouragement. Often discouraged in the home, often at school, often by families and spouses, the rare woman writer who does not lose her determination along the way is already a survivor. That one should next have to face the systematic discouragement of a male-oriented literary establishment is absurd and sad but nonetheless a real fact of life for many women writers.* The truth is that many of us are doomed to do our best work in an atmosphere of condescension and loneliness. Yet perhaps there is some sense in which that lack of establishment approval is a blessing, for an artist must learn (the sooner the better) that he or she works for the work itself, not for approval, and it is easier to establish that sense of creative independence when approval is lacking than when one is seduced by it. Prizes, awards, rave reviews are, after all, snares, and perhaps they are more destructive to one's sense of creative

* No one has chronicled this repression better than Tillie Olsen in her splendid book *Silences* (1978).

independence than the systematic discouragement the per-petual outsider receives. Still, we cannot truly understand the situation of the woman writer unless we are honest about this systematic discouragement, and unless we try to see clearly the form it takes, and the strategies of survival it imposes upon the individual artist. School is as good a place to start as any, for school is a microcosm of our society's values.

One of the most notable (and faintly horrifying) memories from my college years is the time a Distinguished Critic came to my creative writing class and delivered himself of the following thundering judgment: "Women can't be writers. They don't know blood and guts, and puking in the streets, and fucking whores, and swaggering through Pigalle at 5 A.M. ..." But the most amazing thing was the *response*—or lack of it. It was 1961 or '62, and we all sat there—aspiring women writers that we were—and listened to this Maileresque claptrap without a word of protest. Our hands folded on our laps, our eyes modestly downcast, our hearts cast even lower than our eyes, we listened meekly—while the male voice of authority told us what women could or couldn't write.

Things have changed since then. When I went to college (from 1959 to 1963), there were no women's studies courses, no anthologies that stressed a female heritage, no public women's movement. Poetry meant Yeats, Lowell, James Dickey. Without even realizing it, I assumed that the voice of the poet had to be male. Not that I didn't get a good literary education. I did. Barnard was a miraculous place where they actually gave you a degree for losing yourself in a library with volumes of Byron and Keats, Shakespeare and Chaucer, but the whole female side of the library heritage was something I would have to discover for myself years later, propelled by the steam generated by the women's movement.

No Distinguished Critic would dare say such things to a college class today (however much he might think them). Sexism is somewhat better hidden now—though it is far from eradicated. And no college class would sit meekly listening to such rubbish. That is one of the things that has happened in the years since I graduated from college, and I am proud to have been part of the process. Now, when I go to read my work at colleges, I find the students reading and discussing contemporary writing by women as if there never had been a time when a Distinguished Critic could say "Women can't be writers"—even in jest. I am grateful and glad for that change, but it has not been won without pain. Nor is it necessarily a lasting change. Like the feminists of the twenties, we could easily see the interest in female accomplishments once again eclipsed by reactionary sexism, only to have to be passionately rediscovered yet again, several decades later.

It's ironic that Mr. Distinguished Critic should have identified Blood and Guts as the thing that women writers supposedly lacked,* because in the first years of the women's movement, there was so *much* Blood and Guts in women's writing that one wondered if women writers ever did anything but menstruate and rage. Released from the prison of propriety, blessedly released from having to pretend meekness, gratefully in touch with our own cleansing anger, we raged and mocked and menstruated through whole volumes of prose and poetry. This was fine for writers who had a saving sense of irony, but in many cases the rage tended to eclipse the writing. Also, as years went by, literary feminism tended to ossify into convention. Rage became almost as compulsory to the generation of writers who came of age in the late sixties and early seventies as niceness and meekness had been to an earlier generation. Feminists proved that they could be as rigidly dogmatic as any other group. They did not hesitate to criticize works of art on political grounds and

---

* This is indeed a curious metaphor for what women writers supposedly lack, since of course it is obvious that women are the sex most in tune with the entrails of life, as it were. But we can understand the great critic's condemnation better if we remember that in the nineteenth century women writers were denigrated for their delicacy, their excessive propriety (which supposedly precluded greatness), while in the past decade or so they have been condemned by male critics for their *im*propriety—which also supposedly precludes greatness. The whole issue is a red herring. Whatever women writers do or do not do precludes greatness (in the mind of the chauvinist) simply because they are women. We must see this sort of reasoning for what it is: namely, misogyny. See Mary Ellmann's wonderful book, *Thinking about Women* (1968) on the subjects of sexual stereotypes and phallic criticism. She exposes the hypocrisies of phallic criticism with great wit.

to reject poems and novels for dealing with supposedly counterrevolutionary subjects.

This was unfortunate. It was also, I suppose inevitable. Anger against patriarchal stifling of talent had been so proscribed for so many centuries that in letting it loose, many women completely lost their sense of humor. Nor could anyone maintain that getting in touch with anger was unimportant. It was, in fact, a vitally important phase for women's writing to go through. Nothing is more destructive of the spirit and ultimately of creativity than false meekness, anger that does not know its own name. And nothing is more freeing for a woman (or for a woman writer) than giving up the pleasures of masochism and beginning to fight. But we must always remember that fighting is only a first step. As Virginia Woolf points out in *A Room of One's Own*, many women's books have been destroyed by the rage and bitterness at their own centers. Rage opens the doors into the spirit, but then the spirit must be nurtureed. This is hardly easy because women writers (like women) tend to be damned no matter what they do. If we are sweet and tender, we are damned for not being "powerful" enough (not having "blood and guts"), and if we rage, we are said to be "castrating," Amazonian, lacking in tenderness. It is a real dilemma. What is the authentic voice of the woman writer? Does anyone *know?* Does anyone know what the authentic voice of woman is? Is it sweet and low like the voice of Shakespeare's Cordelia, or is it raging and powerful like the voice of Lady Macbeth? Is it an alternation of the two?

The problem is, I suppose, that women have never been left alone to *be* themselves and to find out for themselves. Men need them so badly and are so terrified of losing them that they have used their power to imprison them. To imprison them in castles of stone as long as that was possible, and to imprison them in castles of myth thereafter. The myths were mostly ways of keeping us out of touch with our own strength, and this confused many generations of women. We were told we were weak, yet as we grew older, we increasingly sensed we were strong. We were told that men loved us for our dependency, yet as we grew older, we observed that, despite themselves, they loved us for our independence, and if they didn't—we didn't

always care! We found that we could grow only by loving
ourselves a little, and loving our strengths, and so, paradoxically,
we found we could only grow up by doing the opposite of all the
things our culture told us to do. We were told our charm lay in
weakness; yet in order to survive, we had to be strong. We were
told we were by nature indecisive; and yet, having been told
that, our very existence often seemed to depend on our
decisiveness. We were told that certain mythic definitions of
women were immutable natural laws, biological "facts"; yet so
often our very endurance depended upon changing those
supposedly unchangeable things, and upon embracing a life
credo of change.

In fact, when I look back on the years since I left college, and I
try to sum up what I have learned, it is precisely that: not to fear
change, not to expect my life to be immutable. All the good
things that have happened to me in the last several years have
come, without exception, from a willingness to change, to risk
the unknown, to do the very things I feared the most. Every
poem, every page of fiction I have written, has been written with
anxiety, occasionally panic, always uncertainty about its reception. Every life decision I have made—from changing jobs, to
changing partners, to changing homes—has been taken with
trepidation. I have not ceased being fearful, but I have ceased to
let fear control me. I have accepted fear as a part of life,
specifically the fear of change, the fear of the unknown, and I
have gone ahead despite the pounding in the heart that says: turn
back, turn back, you'll die if you venture too far.

I regard myself as a fairly typical member of the female sex,
and as a fairly typical member of the class of '63. I may have a
greater talent for self-expression, but in my fears and feelings, I
am the same. My talent to write may propel me into places and
situations I wouldn't otherwise find myself in, but in the dark of
night, having insomnia, I think the same thoughts as you or you. I
get impatient with successful women who feel that their success
has lifted them out of the ordinary stream of women's lives and
who say to their fearful, unfledged sisters: I did it against the
odds; you can, too. As a writer, I feel that the very source of my
inspiration lies in my never forgetting how much I have in

common with other women, how many ways in which we are all—successful or not— similarly shackled. I do not write about superwomen who have transcended all conflict; I write about women who are torn, as most of us are torn, between the past and the future, between our mothers' frustrations and the extravagant hopes we have for our daughters. I do not know what a writer would write about if all her characters were superwomen, cleansed of conflict. Conflict is the soul of literature.

I know I would not mind envisioning a world in which my daughter were free *not* to be a feminist,* were free (if she chose to be a writer) not to write about women's conflicts, not to assume that the accident of her gender compelled her work to have a specific creative bias. But I would also like to see a world in which male writers wrote without masculinist bias, in which for example Hemingway's masculinist mythology (and that of many other contemporary American male writers) was perceived as quite as bizarre and hysterical as the most absurd excesses of militant feminist fiction, and in which consciousness had become so truly androgynous that the adjective itself would be puzzlingly obsolete. Alas, I do not think our culture is heading in this direction. I think, rather, that after a brief flirtation with sensitivity to patriarchal attitudes (brought about by what has been termed the "second wave" of the women's movement— roughly that fleeting half-decade from 1969 to 1974) the culture is sliding back into its habitual sexism (with perhaps a few new wrinkles of equality, created more by the birth-control revolution and the ravages of inflation upon the average family income than by feminist theory). Radical feminists have, in a sense, abetted this process of backsliding by becoming quite as simple-mindedly dogmatic as the most dogmatic male chauvinists, by disassociating themselves from the realities of most women's lives: i.e., a desire for children and warm affective relationships with men. It is unrealistic to assume that after living in families

---

* I assume here that feminism is necessitated by our patriarchal culture. In a truly egalitarian culture, feminism would be obsolete. Let us all pray for such obsolescence.

and tribes for millions of years of human evolution, women will suddenly cease to need affective relationships with men and children and become either solitaries or feminist communards. The human need for companionship and sexuality is far stronger than any intellectual theory, and the point is not to keep women from establishing families (a desire that may even be instinctual) but rather to make their *position* in families less that of semislaves and more that of autonomous individuals within the protection of the group.

Where does all this leave the woman writer of our age? Usually in a quandary. As a sharp observer of her society she cannot fail to see that it discriminates against women (often in emotionally crippling and physically murderous ways), but as an artist she cannot allow her vision to be polluted by the ephemeral dogmas of political movements. It is simply not possible to write a good book that "proves" the essential righteousness of either lesbianism or heterosexuality, childbearing or its avoidance, man-loving or man-hating. Righteousness has, in fact, no place in literature. Of course the keen observer of her culture will feel deeply about the oppression she sees around her, the inhumanity of man to man, of man to woman, but her vision of it must be essentially personal, not abstractly political. Books are not written by committees—at least not good books. And the woman writer has as much right as any other artist to an essentially individual and idiosyncratic vision. If we judge her books according to their political "correctness," we are doing her as great a disservice as if we judged them according to her looks or her behavior in the voting booth. Certainly human history is full of such judgmentalism—most of it not coming from women—but always it is antithetical to the creation of works of art.

After saying all of this, I must also gratefully acknowledge that the second wave of the feminist movement liberated my writing and was a liberating influence upon my whole life. How? Not by supplying me with dogma, but by making it easier for me to look into myself and assume that what I felt as a woman was also shared by other women (and men). For one of the most positive by-products of the so-called second wave of the feminist

movement was its discovery of a new audience of readers—
readers both female and male—who came to realize that literary
history as we previously knew it was the history of the literature
of the white, the affluent, the male, and that the female side of
experience had been almost completely omitted (except as seen
through the eyes of the traditional victors in the war between
the sexes*—men). And this audience was suddenly passionately
interested in dispatches from the center of the female heart
which represented a sort of dark continent, a *terra incognita*,
the exploration of which was necessary to a full understanding
of human consciousness in all its permutations.

From the courage the women's movement gave and from the
reinforcement I received from grateful and passionate readers, I
learned the daring to assume that my thoughts, nightmares, and
daydreams were the same as my readers'. I discovered that
whenever I wrote about a fantasy I thought was wholly private,
bizarre, kinky—the fantasy of the Zipless Fuck in *Fear of Flying*
is perhaps the best example of this—I invariably discovered that
thousands of other people had experienced the same private,
bizarre, and kinky fantasy.

In the past several years, I have learned, in short, to trust
myself. Not to eradicate fear but to go on in spite of fear. Not to
become insensitive to distinguished critics but to follow my own
writer's instinct despite what they say women should or should
not write. My job is not to paralyze myself by anticipating
judgment but to do the best I can and let the judgment fall
where it may. The difference between the woman who is writing
this essay and the girl sitting in that creative writing class in
1961 is mostly a matter of nerve and daring—the nerve to trust
my own instincts and the daring to be a fool. No one ever found

---

* The question of whether or not men are really victors in the war between the
sexes is older than Aristophanes' *Lyistrata*. In terms of the distribution of
society's material goodies and power, they are clearly victors, but there is
much reason to believe that their very status as victors has robbed them
emotionally—and robbed them of the sort of flexibility and emotional
openness women more usually possess. Still, this is the price they pay for their
own dominance, and the fact that the underdog has certain emotional
advantages should never obscure the fact that she *is* the underdog.

wisdom without also being a fool. Writers, alas, have to be fools in public, while the rest of the human race can cover its tracks. But it is also painfully true that no one avoids being a fool without also avoiding growth, and growth does not, alas, stop with the current feminist vision of reality. It goes on far beyond it.

It seems to me that having now created an entire literature of female rage, an entire literature of female introspection, women writers are ready to enter the next phase—the phase of empathy. Without forgetting how hard-won our rage was, without forgetting how many puritanical voices would still like to censor our sexuality, I think we must consider ourselves free to explore the whole world of feeling in our writings—and not to be trapped forever in the phase of discovering buried anger. The anger has been discovered, unearthed, anatomized, and catalogued. It may be a strong propellant to the creation of literature, but it is hardly the only propellant. Stronger even than anger is curiosity—motional and intellectual curiosity—the vehicles through which we enter into other states of being, other lives, other historical periods, other galaxies. Patriarchy will have truly crippled women if it prevents us from experiencing our native human curiosity (because that curiosity has been so overlaid with rage at our position in society). The time has come to let go of that rage; the time has come to realize that curiosity is braver than rage, that exploration is a nobler calling than war. As artists, the unknown beckons to us, singing its siren song and making our hearts pound with fear and desire. Let us not tie ourselves to the mast of anger but sail into the unknown, fearful of the future, yet not paralyzed into immobility by fear; *feeling* the fear, yet not letting the fear control us. This is the ultimate test of our blood and guts. Those who pass it will discover new worlds and create a new literature by women truly worthy of our courage, our imagination, and our craft.

JAN MORRIS

TRAVELLING WRITER

IN my heart I resist the title of this book, or rather its implication: namely that it matters whether a writer is male or female. I believe the fount of art to be beyond gender, just as I believe the human soul itself to be housed in a particular physique merely for practical purposes of reproduction—slotted along the continuum that is, in my view, the true measure of sex. The so-called war between the sexes seems to me a trumped-up conflict, presently to be resolved: and I suspect that the very distinction between masculine and feminine will one day be of purely functional significance.

But having lived my own life partly as a man, partly as a woman, I recognize of course how powerfully, in our own time, the circumstance of gender affects one's work as a writer: and I admit that at the core of everything I have done myself, somewhere between the lines of all my books, lies the fact of my own particular and peculiar status in the present state of sex.

Take for a start the workaday, humdrum aspects of the writer's life. I am a travelling writer—not a travel writer, a category I reject, but a writer who travels. That I write about place is almost incidental to my vocation. I am really an essayist, often of an all too protracted kind, but it so happens that the Second World War, by making me a traveller whether I wanted it or not, provided me with a particular range of subject matter—the matter of place, which I have manipulated ever since in works of memoir, description, history, and fiction. If chance had given me a more domestic role in life, I have no doubt that the basic material of my essays would have been altogether different, and I might have launched myself from the start into miniatures or abstractions.

Be that as it may, destiny made me a travelling writer, with all the addictions that such a calling implies: restless addictions, footloose addictions, a taste for the solitary, and an appetite for things colorful, quirky, and exciting. After the British Army and Oxford University I spent a decade as a foreign correspondent, and this soon instilled in me, as it instills in most practitioners of the trade, a cynical disregard for fame, power, and consequence: but it also disqualified me once and for all for the routines and preoccupations of life at home.

So I wander always, torn between the places I love the best of all, my own corner of Wales, and the kaleidoscopic variety of everywhere else: between the people I love the best, my family, and the inexhaustible allure of new faces, languages, styles, and manners of thought. It is a *wrenched* kind of life, a perpetual dichotomy, a periodical trauma, but I am certainly not complaining: if this is neurosis, you can keep your normalcy.

It is however a demanding existence, stressful and just occasionally dangerous, and at literary festivals especially I am often asked if it has become easier for me, or more difficult, since I made my shift along the gauge of sex. In some ways, I have to reply, more difficult, because physically it is obviously riskier, even now, for a woman to travel alone in the world with the intention of writing about it. One is more vulnerable than a man, more conspicuous too, and technically this has sometimes been a handicap to me. Aspects of life that I was once free to explore are now more generally denied me, and I have occasionally regretted it, when the dim lights and loud music of a dubious tavern beckon, or I am disbarred from entering some fascinatingly old-school club.

But not often. I have hated nightlife always, and seldom in fact pine for leather-backed chairs and gentlemanly tradition. Besides, I set against these lesser disadvantages the assets of travelling as a woman. The chief and most obvious of these is the fact that among the human species, as among most of the animals, the female is not generally perceived as threatening. Novelists and New Yorkers may scoff, but in general it is true, and the solitary woman traveller raises far fewer suspicions, finds far fewer doors closed against her, than does a wandering man.

More positively, too, the woman travelling writer can know that more than half of humanity is likely to be actually on her side—cheering her on! When Kipling wrote about "sisters under the skin," he was in his allusive way enunciating a great truth: that on the whole—and God knows, with exceptions—women are kinder to women than men are to men. You must take my word for this, as one who has experienced both relationships, and you must believe me too that for a writer especially this grand freemasonry around the world infinitely outweighs a woman's vulnerability as a traveller.

Twenty years ago I would have said that on the other hand the woman was hampered by male inability to take her seriously. I used to feel it myself, when I first began to travel as a woman, and found my opinions disregarded and my questions patronizingly set aside. No longer. It is the great triumph of the feminist movement that the intellectual equality of women is now all but universally recognized (if not invariably, especially when it comes to equal pay or opportunity, admitted ...).

Anyway all this is ancillary to the writer's craft and purpose, which is above all self-generating and internal. I don't believe a sensibility depends upon gender, and I think I write in the way I write not because I am male, female, both, or neither, but simply because I am myself: *"le style est l'homme même,"* said de Buffon long ago, but he meant *l'homme*, I do not doubt, in shorthand for humanity.

Sensibility however is a different thing from experience, and the experience of our gender, while it may not affect our style, certainly affects our responses. In my own case the anomalies of my sex have powerfully affected, without doubt, the way I have looked at the world, besides the way I have lived in it. I expect in some respects they have distorted or weakened my reactions, but I prefer to look upon the bright side, and contemplate their benefits instead.

I think they made me, from the start, one of life's outsiders. This would be a weakness for writers of other kinds, but it has been good for me. The essence of my work, whether it deals with the past or the present, whether it is fact or fiction, is detachment—not alienation or estrangement, merely standing separate. Actually detachment of a kind is endemic to the tradition of English writing to which I feel myself, though actually Anglo-Welsh, to belong: the classic detachment of the English abroad, amounting very nearly to aloofness and exemplified in the work of such masters of my own genre as Emily Eden or Alexander Kinglake. American writers about place have more generally felt the urge to get within the skin of the people they are observing: English writers have preferred to watch from a safe distance, through a screen of irony.

More fundamentally, and conversely, I like to think my peculiar sexuality has widened my empathies. If I feel separate from everyone, I feel close to everyone too. Starting with men and women, many of whose varied emotions I have actually shared, I have been able, as I grow older, to extend my range of fellow-feeling: to animals, for instance, to nations, even to inanimate objects. I believe in the absolute equality before God of all living things, slug to dolphin. I do not recognize the crime of treason, having long ago reached the conclusion that nationality, like loyalty, should be purely a matter of choice. I do not feel in the least foolish in apologizing to a table, if I trip over its leg, or jollying along a recalcitrant automobile with encouraging words.

There is a smugness to these attitudes, I know, and a sentimentality too: but then the faults of a writer, as well as the virtues, contribute for better or for worse to the nature of her art.

And on the whole, smug, sentimental, or just a little crazy, I feel myself to be a kind of portent. I believe the conjunction of my self and my work to be a sign of reconciliation—a minuscule sign, Heaven knows, and one apparent perhaps only to myself, but still to my mind a promise of things to come. Long ago the philosopher Teilhard de Chardin conceived the idea of "infurling," an infinitely slow, almost imperceptible coming together of the world and its beings. I see in myself and my work one all but imperceptible confirmation of his vision: and I believe that in a couple of centuries, when people read this book, they will wonder at the primitive nature of our own times, when art could still be collated with gender at all.

ELIZABETH JOLLEY

DIPT ME IN INK

... what sin to me unknown dipt me in ink ...

I always thought I came from a family of no consequence but looking back I remember that when I was about eight years old my father invented heat and light. He wrote two textbooks for school children. The one on heat had a red cover and the one on light was blue. As for inheritance, what fool would claim, ticking the appropriate boxes on the application form for an exclusive school of nursing, a grandpa who died of blood poisoning following severe scalding from the freshly boiled kettle he was carrying when he fell in his last epileptic fit. Then there was the other grandpa who must have owned a disease which, though not acute for himself, destroyed my mother's mother and subsequently three stepmothers. (My mother grew up in a convent.) Aunt Maud and a mysterious cousin called Dorothy were talked about in whispers. Both were said to be mad. Who would acknowledge—with irresponsible ticks—the grand-fathers, the aunt, and the cousin?

The wartime St. Thomas's Hospital, evacuated to smaller hospitals in Surrey, was originally the place where Florence Nightingale made nursing into a profession for ladies. Ladies abounded. One of the probationers (the name for student nurses then) was the daughter of a member of the British War Cabinet. She never had any of the regulation black woolen stockings and was adept at borrowing. But the application form. In addition to the confessions about disease and mental health, the question was asked: *How many maids does your mother keep?* Recalling my mother bent over the sink or the gas boiler I conjured images of devout women with peaceful honest faces, capable hands, and comforting bosoms and I wrote *two* on the form and was accepted. Sometimes I think lovingly of these two maids, dressing them in neat black dresses and the traditional spotless white caps and aprons. One of them, devoted to me and fond of sewing, filled my wardrobe which in truth had nothing in it except my school winter coat, a garment of such sterling quality that it accompanied me, belonging to no fashion, during all the years of the war and longer.

What kind of marriage can spring from the moving sight of Goethe's Werther first observing the youthful and charming Lotte distributing slices of bread at dusk to the small children in her care? My father first beheld my mother in a similar pose but in very different circumstances. She was sharing out soup and bread between her near starving pupils in a school in Vienna. A deeply moving scene but not a good guide to marriage. My father was in Vienna as a relief worker with the Quakers immediately after the First World War. He was distributing food and clothes.

Clytemnestra tells Electra that a daughter can never know and understand the previous experience of the mother.

> ... I agree, one should not speak
> Bitterly. But when people judge someone,
> they ought
> To learn the facts, and then hate, if they've
> reason to
> And if they find no reason, then they should
> not hate.

When I was twelve my mother gave me a little needlebook she had made. Perhaps she hoped the loving verse embroidered on the cover would express her tenderness in some way. I still have the book and perhaps! understand now, too late, something of her hopes and of her suffering.

If I have always been on the edge, something of an exile—not being a Birth Right Quaker at a Quaker boarding school; being a nurse in training alongside girls from *good* families, that is, country families where twin sets and pearls were not just a joke; later in life being a newcomer to Australia where, though the language is the same, the climate and customs are very different—this comes in part, too, from an earlier sense of being on the edge and the feeling of exile experienced by my mother and father. Perhaps my experience of homesickness and exile starts, without any knowledge or understanding, from early memories of incomprehensible unhappiness.

At the age of eleven I was sent to boarding school. Unaccustomed to being with other children and missing the Midlands smell of the bone and glue factory and the heave and roar of the blast furnaces, I cried. Between autumn-berried hedgerows I cried in the middle of a road which seemed to be leading nowhere. I began to write stories at school, perhaps to overcome the pain of homesickness. Homesickness seems to be bitter and wasteful but, of course, all experience, in the end, is useful, especially for the writer.

Is there any way in which a writer can see herself from outside? Probably not. The nearest approach is to try and see how she has become what she is:

> Why did I write? What sin to me unknown
> Dipt me in ink, my parents or my own?

It would seem that all writers draw heavily on their early experience but in different ways. Some directly but perhaps some more indirectly. One thinks of Tolstoy, Wordsworth, Traherne. The experience may be happy or unhappy. Which it is does not alter its influence. It might be thought that Gorky and Dickens might have obliterated all memory of their childhoods!

My mother and father were married in Vienna soon after the Great War which ended in defeat and destruction of the Habsburg Empire. Vienna was no longer the administrative center of a large empire. My mother's father (the grandpa who had four wives) had been a general in the Imperial Army; he belonged to the great number of people whose reason for existence disappeared with the emperor.

My father with his fine white teeth and thick hair suggested, in his appearance, a life in England which would restore prosperity and social status. My mother confessed later to imagining that she would live in a large country house set in its own park. The England of her hopes did not turn out to be as expected. My father was a teacher in the heart of England's Industrial Midlands, the Black Country, an area of coal mines, brickworks, iron and steel foundries, factories, and rows of mean little houses in narrow streets.

Because of her marriage my mother was an exile. I remember that her homesickness lasted throughout her life. It was a longing for a homeland as it had been and not for what it had become.

My father loved my mother very much and always spoke German at home. German was the language of the household even though my mother spoke English fluently—with a Viennese accent and intonation. At the age of six when I started school, surrendering to my surroundings, I stopped speaking German.

My father's exile came about because of his ideals. During the Great War he suffered brutal imprisonment as a conscientious objector. His father (the grandfather who scalded himself) disowned him, turning him out of the house in front of the gathered neighbors, because of his beliefs and the disgrace of being in prison. He returned from Vienna bringing a wife, an impoverished aristocrat, to his father's house from an enemy country. When speaking about this later he was not bitter about his father but he did say that he felt for many years, because of the experience, that he had been "warped." He said, too, that one of the things about being in prison was that there was no grass and there were no flowers. He was never able to face cocoa or porridge because of the time in prison. Though, with his face averted, he made both for us when we were children. It was as if he were trying to offer an apology when he talked shyly of those times. He wept during the declaration of the Second World War because he could not believe that the same kind of cruelties would be carried out all over again. One of the things which had shocked him in 1914 was the excitement and eager anticipation for "bloodshed" among the people crowding the streets. It was as if they needed this excitement, as if their ordinary lives were too dull. In 1939 he stood on street corners giving away copies of *Peace News*. He said it was sad that people needed a war to make them feel neighborly; drawn together because it was a time of disaster. I went unwillingly and handed out *Peace News*. I am glad now that I stood with him and I have since been deeply ashamed of my unwillingness. I was brought up at home and at school to feel that all war is wrong.

My novel *Milk and Honey* contains the shadows and the weeping of people my mother and father tried to help before and during the second war. Many refugees came to our house and often my sister and I slept on the sofa or the floor because there were people who needed our beds.

During my childhood we lived in a neighborhood curious about and hostile to foreigners. My father, containing in himself conflicts between science (his subject), human effort, and what is called religion, took us away from school when I was eight. In spite of being a teacher he thought school spoiled childhood innocence. We had lessons at home with a series of French and Austrian governesses. Perhaps the wireless lessons were the most successful. Images sprang from the quality and the tone of voice whether the voice was describing the affairs of Parliament, the dangers of unwashed clothes and milk jugs, the circulation of the blood, or the plight of the *Flying Dutchman*. Because we did not go to school and because German was spoken at home we were exiles in our own street. We retreated into fantasy. Our childhood was one long game of people. We were each other's nephews. "I'm her nephew," I told the postmistress, "and she's my nephew." With sofa cushions on our heads we said we were widows. The date-box buses we pushed round on the linoleum stopped at the table legs to pick up the waiting passengers, the little china pigs and dogs and cats, brought by relatives who travelled, and an assortment of wooden clothes pegs hand-painted to look like sailors and Spanish dancers.

Then there were the dolls' houses side by side, opened so that the rooms and lives within were all revealed. In the magic of these openings, the game was an endless story of our own composing from one day to the next for years ...

I am not attempting a self-analysis. The household which presented itself to me as both strange and normal encouraged me to observe. My mother was given to moods. Storms blew up unexpectedly, were savage, and disappeared again as quickly. The governesses departed abruptly, in tears, leaning on my father's arm as he escorted them in turn to the railway station. I became by nature and circumstance a placator and learned to read every change in the eye, every crease in the brow. I am still a placator. Other people's households, if I am a guest, inadvertently trouble me and in my own house I am not able to work if there is some problem or unhappiness which needs sorting out or comforting. The best time for me to write is when other people are asleep. I am not needed in their dreams. I have developed the habit of writing for some hours during the night, working from the quick notes made during the day.

I cannot explain why I am a fiction writer unless the explanation comes in part from a response to my experience of the world in which I grew up and to the strange new world in which we exist today. I do not maintain that a writer should conceal her private life. What must come first are the words, which must not be twisted to fit some preconceived image of the writer. Sometimes what is most important after infancy is the experience which finds expression only in writing. It is the word which is not spoken, the resolve which is not kept, which become a part of the created. It is as if these things emerge from hidden pathways in an unexpected form. Writing fiction is not easy for me; to write facts is almost impossible.

There is an excitement in exploring characters and in seeing how they react with each other in different situations. I have always kept diaries and journals ever since I was a child. Lately I have noticed that I do not want to write in the journal because of a feeling that I am encouraging sad thoughts and increasing anxiety by dwelling at length on troublesome things and writing about them. I prefer now to retain the ability to make the quick note of truth and awareness, to notice some small thing about a person, a stranger—perhaps someone choosing knitting wool in the supermarket, something like that—and move into imaginative fiction from the small truthful moment, the little picture, the idea which is so slender it hardly seems to matter. And then suddenly I am exploring human feelings and reasons.

I do not think I lack social awareness. When I look back at my earlier writing, I find themes which were then mostly avoided but are now widely discussed. Imaginative writing can increase awareness but it cannot demonstrate the need for specific programs. When I write "I" in a story or a novel I do not mean I—myself. Some people have been disappointed that I am not any one or all of my characters.

Sometimes a childhood memory becomes suddenly vivid and powerful without it being written down. One of these was a game which my father described one evening when he was making our cocoa. I suppose I must have been about five or six years old. I liked to hear things about him. He and his sister (my aunt) played a game called horses and carts, he told us; they played on the kitchen table with an assortment of screws and nails and small nuts and bolts. The table was the street and the nuts and bolts and things went up and down, to and fro, fast and slow on the table; they were the horses and carts and that is how they played. In between games the screws and nails and things were kept in a jar with a screw-top lid.

More than fifty years later, having the sound still in my head, I gave the game to a character:

> We're running still, lightly now, one foot—two foot—one foot—two foot—foot—foot—foot—breathe in breathe out breathe in. Side by side we're running, easily.
>
> "What about the kitchen table?" he asks me. "Where did yer put yer nuts and bolts?" His breathing's easier. "Where'd you put yer horses and carts of a night time?"
>
> "I knew you'd ask that," I say. "I'll tell you. My dad made me a bit of a table out of an old box in the trailer and every night I set out my horses and carts, dot—dot—dotty—dot—up and down, to and fro along the road, fast and slow, my horses and carts passed each other, stopped to let each other go by, they turned into the roadway and sometimes they collided."

The boy's game as he plays it while his father looks on parallels some of the action in the story.

The strange thing is that my sister, who is about a year younger than I am, does not remember my father describing the horses and carts game.

In my childhood there were enrichments which at the time did not seem particularly enriching. People played the piano and sang Schubert *Lieder*. My father sat with one hand shading his eyes but I saw his tears. Then the music changed and someone sang *How do you feel when you marry your ideal Ever so goosey goosey goosey*. And someone else sang "The Wedding of the Painted Doll." My mother danced twirling her beads, strings of them; she danced kicking her feet out to the sides, heels up, toes down and turned in. Across the room she danced, across the room and back. How can it be explained that these pictures of those times and the songs which I never thought about for years came back to me to be a part of a short story?

Music is important to me. Certain passages of music, whenever I hear them, recreate certain characters. I seem to see the characters again and again as I once saw them when first writing about them. It seems that music helps me to show greater depths in the creating of the characters through the effect music has on them. Daphne in the novel *The Sugar Mother* plays an ancient record of the Indian love call from *Hiawatha* in the bathroom before a scene which she intends to be erotic. Edwin Page, in the same novel, remembers a Mozart piano concerto which suggests to him a fault in the music which is there on purpose and is put right. He says he can hear the going back over the notes and then the going forward in correction. To him this suggests that there can be a fault in life which can be put right in the same manner, but Daphne points out that this is not so. The music does not go back to allow for correction but presses on in the way it was going. A parallel for events in Edwin's life? Edwin is the hopeful dreamer and Daphne is seen to be the outspoken realist.

My character Miss Hailey, in the novel *Mr. Scobie's Riddle*, grew from the sight of a woman in an unusual straw hat. That was all I noticed about her when passing her in the street. When I made a note about the hat, at home, I imagined how pleased the woman in the hat (Miss Hailey) would be to be able to tell someone the way. Later when I discovered that Miss Hailey had the horns from *Eroica* stored within her I began to know more and more about her.

Hester Harper in the novel *The Well* is aware that while she listens to Mozart she changes from being the severe woman she is by reputation:

She knew from listening alone that while she listened her mouth took on a different shape, the lips drawn together and pursed ... she understood the possibility that her whole body was, during the music, different. Without meaning to she knew it was not only her lips; it was all the seriousness and tenderness which entered and set the bones of her jaw and changed the movement of her eyebrows and the tilt of her head ...

I do not know if this is an interesting fact but I am the sort of person who needs to create a superficial order in my surroundings before I can confront the confusion which exists in my mind and in the scattered notes I gather over days, weeks, months, and years for the making of a story or a novel. I have to know in advance what I am going to prepare for the family dinner. I like to have the essentials of housework done and correspondence answered before working at the novel—if I am going to work during the day. I find it very hard to emerge from the fiction to an uncared-for house. The move from the desk to the domestic, toward the end of an afternoon, is one of the most painful experiences. I do not think this is hard for women only, but perhaps women more often find themselves in this position even in these times when women are "liberated"—and in spite of the washing machine and the dishwasher.

I never write a synopsis or an outline. If I did I might lose the idea before it was born. The language of the synopsis might kill the energy and rhythm of the special writing needed for the story. I often wish that in writing I could start with the first words and move smoothly on and on to the last words. Writing for me is a ragged and restless activity with scattered fragments to be pieced together rather like a patchwork quilt. I rewrite a great deal and usually write the first pages last and often put off writing the end for a long time. I cannot explain any of this.

I came to Western Australia from Britain in the middle of my life. I realize that the freshness of my observation can distort as well as illuminate. The impact of the new country does not obliterate the previous one but sharpens memory, thought, and feeling thus providing a contrasting theme or setting. There are advantages in having several landscapes. In the novel *Miss Peabodys Inheritance* I make use of several backgrounds—Britain, Europe, and

Western Australia. Conveniently there can be details of journeys and places visited en route. The landscape of my writing is not to be found clearly on any map. The light and shade of a particular tree or the effect of water on a paddock at a particular moment may be used. In the story "Two Men Running" one of the men, longing for his destroyed life to become whole again, talks to his companion about aspects of his life and an awareness which he usually keeps hidden:

> "The gravel pits, the hills, the catchment and the foxgloves in the catchment. Did you know," I ask him. "Did you know that where water collects and runs off the rocks there are different flowers growing there? Did you know that because of this water, a paddock can be deep purple like a plum? And then, if you think about plums, the different colours range from deep purple through to the pale pearly green of the translucent satsuma before it ripens. Because of water that's how a paddock can look from one end to the other. It's the same with people ..."

In writing the above I was trying to show something of my character's need to re-create the wholesomeness of the landscape of his childhood. A consolation in his time of trouble.

It used to be the fashion, or perhaps there was a need, for Western Australian writers to deny their region. Some years ago an editor told me that I was *revealing* the Western Australian setting in a novel by putting in jarrah trees and the fact that looking westward it was possible to see the sea. The editor's geography was not foolproof, for there are other places in Australia from which the sea can be seen westward. I kept the offending details in the novel. Characters and themes are often universal and the landscape and setting from the writer's own region can bring to the work a particular flavor. In Western Australia, in the vastness of this one-third of the whole continent, there are a variety of regions. Travelling inland in an easterly direction from the seashore there are the suburbs, the city, the sand plains, and the wide valley of the Swan River where the vineyards lie in neat patterns, a well-made patchwork. Then there are the escarpment, bush and semi-rural land, more bush—partly cleared for horses and sheep—and then the wheat country for miles to the rabbitproof fence beyond which lies one of the great deserts.

For some years I have been teaching in the English Department at Curtin University of Technology, Perth. I teach, too, in the prisons and in the remote country districts. I think that teaching, like nursing, helps writing. Certainly working with people does not hamper the writer. I often make long journeys alone by car to remote wheat towns and farms. Sometimes during these long drives I stop the car and walk for a while at the side of the long straight road, low down between the paddocks which stretch endlessly on both sides of far-away horizons. A practical consideration which brought me into a new perspective was the realization that nowadays a tiny handful of unseen people produce from the vast landscape enormous quantities of food. I find that I like to feel small and insignificant on one of these empty roads with the great dome of the familiar sky above, a floating roof of light clear air. I have given Hester Harper in the novel *The Well* this same experience and feeling, though I am not Hester and my life has never been like hers.

The landscape can be used to parallel the attitudes and feelings of my characters. At the beginning of the novel *Foxybaby*, Miss Porch sets off on a long lonely drive to a distant and remote place where she is to be a drama tutor in a summer school:

There is only one road going east from the township of Cheathem West and this road after approximately two hours of sedate driving (one hour for the reckless) becomes the main high street of Cheathem East.

There are scarcely any houses in Cheathem East as very few people live there. There is no hotel and no shop.

Scattered between the two Cheathems are a few lonely farms tucked and folded as if sewn neatly into the landscape for many years. In places, where the road rises, the dark seams of these farms can be seen in the distance. It is as if they are embroidered with rich green wool or silk on a golden background. In the design of the embroidery are a few trees and some silent houses and sheds. Narrow places, fenced off and watered sparingly, produce a little more of the dark-green effect in the picture.

At intervals, sometimes as if they do not belong to anyone in particular, there are unsupervised windmills turning and clicking with a kind of solemn and honest obedience.

Miss Porch journeys all day toward her last hour of driving through a landscape which seems to be without people. I was able to use the silence of this landscape as a contrast to the bizarre crowd of noisy people she encounters at the school.

Western Australian writers no longer hide their region. The climate of acceptance has changed dramatically in Australia during the last decade. Contemporary fiction and poetry are able to reflect with accuracy the landscape and the society in which the writer lives. There is an audience now for the strong voices from a greater number of women writers.

Over the years it has become clear to me that I am deeply interested in people. I am curious about their motives, their feelings, their ambitions, and their hopes and disappointments. It seems to me that every person is a kind of miracle in both the anatomy and the physiology. A miracle, too, in the use of the mind, the intelligence, the memory, and the emotions— unbelievably miraculous. To study and to write about the manifestation of human life, to create characters and situations from the observation of real life is a great privilege. In spite of the excitement and the sense of privilege, writing is, for me, an act of the will.

I want, in my writing, to be optimistic and fond.

The fiction writer has the opportunity to offer people something entertaining but, at the same time, might be able to change a person's outlook on life or their direction, perhaps toward the more loving and optimistic—in spite of the often grim vision of the writer. All sides of human life can be looked upon.

I think people need cherishing. Perhaps the ability to cherish and to feel cherished in adult life comes, in part, from the forgotten experience of the cherishing, the love and the hopes, poured upon the child by the mother and the father, the grandmother and grandfather.

In the novel *Tess of the D'Urbervilles* Hardy describes the Durbeyfield children as being passengers in the Durbeyfield ship, depending on their parents for everything:

If the heads of the Durbeyfield household chose to sail into difficulty, disaster, starvation, disease, degradation, death, thither were these half-dozen little captives under hatches compelled to sail with them ...

Because of being under the hatches of my father's beliefs, his ideals and his innocence, I have had certain experiences which might be thought to be unusual. One of these was my being in Germany at a time when people, without my father's optimism, would not have considered being in that country. I was in a German schoolgirls' camp about fifteen miles from Hamburg during the summer of 1939. The summer camp ended abruptly for me when I was rushed in an unreliable car to the docks and pushed onto a small ship, a cargo boat bound for Hull. I lay on the deck, seasick and surrounded by baskets and baskets of bilberries. As it turned out, it was the last boat to leave for Britain. Had I not made the bilberry basket journey just then, my life might have been very different.

I have never considered this before, but I think I alternate between optimism and anxiety. I realize that should either of these get out of hand I would probably need a clever doctor. This writing about myself and my work, this self-examination disturbs me. I would prefer to be trying to write fiction.

The best thing about writing books, for me, is when a stranger comes up to me in the supermarket and tells me about one of the books and how it was either disliked or liked. Sometimes the book being described is only partly one of mine and mostly someone else's. But that doesn't really matter ...

MARGARET WALKER

ON BEING FEMALE, BLACK,
AND FREE

MY birth certificate reads female, Negro, date of birth and place. Call it fate or circumstance, this is my human condition. I have no wish to change it from being female, black, and free. I like being a woman. I have a proud black heritage, and I have learned from the difficult exigencies of life that freedom is a philosophical state of mind and existence. The mind is the only place where I can exist and feel free. In my mind I am absolutely free.

My entire career of writing, teaching, lecturing, yes, and raising a family is determined by these immutable facts of my human condition. As a daughter, a sister, a sweetheart, a wife, a mother, and now a grandmother, my sex or gender is pre-eminent, important, and almost entirely deterministic. Maybe my glands have something to do with my occupation as a creative person. About this, I am none too sure, but I think the cycle of life has much to do with the creative impulse and the biorhythms of life must certainly affect everything we do.

Creativity cannot exist without the feminine principle, and I am sure God is not merely male or female but He-She—our Father-Mother God. All nature reflects this rhythmic and creative principle of feminism and femininity: the sea, the earth, the air, fire, and all life whether plant or animal. Even as they die, are born, grow, reproduce, and grow old in their cyclic time, so do we in lunar, solar, planetary cycles of meaning and change.

Ever since I was a little girl I have wanted to write and I have been writing. My father told my mother it was only a puberty urge and would not last, but he encouraged my early attempts at rhyming verses just the same, and he gave me the notebook or daybook in which to keep my poems together. When I was eighteen and had ended my junior year in college, my father laughingly agreed it was probably more than a puberty urge. I had filled the 365 pages with poems.

Writing has always been a means of expression for me and for other black Americans who are just like me, who feel, too, the need for freedom in this "home of the brave, and land of the free." From the first, writing meant learning the craft and developing the art. Going to school had one major goal, to learn to be a writer. As early as my eighth year I had the desire, at ten I was trying, at eleven and twelve I was learning, and at fourteen and fifteen I was seeing my first things printed in local school and community papers. I have a copy of a poem published in 1930 and an article with the caption, "What Is to Become of Us?" which appeared in 1931 or 1932. All of this happened before I went to Northwestern.

I spent fifteen years becoming a poet before my first book appeared in 1942. I was learning my craft, finding my voice, seeking discipline as life imposes and superimposes that discipline upon the artist. Perhaps my home environment was most important in the early stages—hearing my mother's music, my sister and brother playing the piano, reading my father's books, hearing his sermons, and trying every day to write a poem. Meanwhile, I found I would have to start all over again and learn how to write prose fiction in order to write the novel I was determined to create to the best of my ability and thus fulfill my promise to my grandmother. A novel is not written exactly the same way as a poem, especially a long novel and a short poem. The creative process may be basically the same—that is, the thinking or conceptualization—but the techniques, elements, and form or craft are decidedly and distinctively different.

It has always been my feeling that writing must come out of living, and the writer is no more than his personality endures in the crucible of his times. As a woman, I have come through the fires of hell because I am a black woman, because I am poor, because I live in America, and because I am determined to be both a creative artist and maintain my inner integrity and my instinctive need to be free.

I don't think I noticed the extreme discrimination against

women while I was growing up in the South. The economic struggle to exist and the racial dilemma occupied all my thinking until I was more than an adult woman. My mother had undergone all kinds of discrimination in academia because of her sex; so have my sisters. Only after I went back to school and earned a doctorate did I begin to notice discrimination against me as a woman. It seems the higher you try to climb, the more rarefied the air, the more obstacles appear. I realize I had been naïve, that the issues had not been obvious and that as early as my first employment I felt the sting of discrimination because I am female.

I think it took the women's movement to call my attention to cases of overt discrimination that hark back to my WPA days on the Writers' Project. It did not occur to me that Richard Wright as a supervisor on the project made $125 per month and that he claimed no formal education, but that I had just graduated from Northwestern University and I was a junior writer making $85 per month. I had no ambitions to be an administrator; I was too glad to have a job; I did not think about it. Now I remember the intense antagonism on the project toward the hiring of a black woman as a supervisor, none other than the famous Katherine Dunham, the dancer, but it never occurred to me then that she was undergoing double discrimination.

When I first went to Iowa and received my master's degree that year there were at least five or six women teaching English in the university. When I returned to study for the doctorate, not a single woman was in the department. At Northwestern my only woman teacher had taught personal hygiene. I did not expect to find women at Yale, but it slowly dawned on me that black women in black colleges were more numerous than white women in coed white universities.

And then I began looking through the pages of books of American and English literature that I was teaching, trying in vain to find the works of many women writers. I have read so many of those great women writers of the world—poets, novelists, and playwrights: Sigrid Undset and Selma Lagerlof, Jane Austen, George Sand, George Eliot, and Colette. All through the ages women have been writing and publishing, black and white

women in America and all over the world. A few women stand
out as geniuses of their times, but those are all too few. Even the
women who survive and are printed, published, taught and
studied in the classroom fall victim to negative male literary
criticism. Black women suffer damages at the hands of every
male literary critic, whether he is black or white. Occasionally a
man grudgingly admits that some woman writes well, but only
rarely.

Despite severe illness and painful poverty, and despite jobs
that always discriminated against me as a woman—never paying
me equal money for equal work, always threatening or replacing
me with a man or men who were neither as well educated nor
experienced but just men—despite all these examples of discrimination I have managed to work toward being a self-
fullfilling, re-creating, reproducing woman, raising a family,
writing poetry, cooking food, doing all the creative things I
know how to do and enjoy. But my problems have not been
simple; they have been manifold. Being female, black, and poor
in America means I was born with three strikes against me. I am
considered at the bottom of the social class-caste system in these
United States, born low on the totem pole. If "a black man has no
rights that a white man is bound to respect," what about a black
woman?

Racism is so extreme and so pervasive in our American society
that no black individual lives in an atmosphere of freedom. The
world of physical phenomena is dominated by fear and greed. It
consists of pitting the vicious and the avaricious against the
naïve, the hunted, the innocent, and the victimized. Power
belongs to the strong, and the strong are BIG in more ways than
one. No one is more victimized in this white male American
society than the black female.

There are additional barriers for the black woman in
publishing, in literary criticism, and in promotion of her literary
wares. It is an insidious fact of racism that the most highly
intellectualized, sensitized white person is not always perceptive
about the average black mind and feeling, much less the
creativity of any black genius. Racism forces white humanity to
underestimate the intelligence, emotion, and creativity of black

humanity. Very few white Americans are conscious of the myth about race that includes the racial stigmas of inferiority and superiority. They do not understand its true economic and political meaning and therefore fail to understand its social purpose. A black, female person's life as a writer is fraught with conflict, competitive drives, professional rivalries, even danger, and deep frustrations. Only when she escapes to a spiritual world can she find peace, quiet, and hope of freedom. To choose the life of a writer, a black female must arm herself with a fool's courage, foolhardiness, and serious purpose and dedication to the art of writing, strength of will and integrity, because the odds are always against her. The cards are stacked. Once the die is cast, however, there is no turning back.

In the first place, the world of imagination in which the writer must live is constantly being invaded by the enemy, the mundane world. Even as the worker in the fires of imagination finds that the world around her is inimical to intellectual activity, to the creative impulse, and to the kind of world in which she must daily exist and also thrive and produce, so, too, she discovers that she must meet that mundane world head-on every day on its own terms. She must either conquer or be conquered.

A writer needs certain conditions in which to work and create art. She needs a piece of time; a peace of mind; a quiet place; and a private life.

Early in my life I discovered I had to earn my living and I would not be able to eke out the barest existence as a writer. Nobody writes while hungry, sick, tired, and worried. Maybe you can manage with one of these but not all four at one time. Keeping the wolf from the door has been my full-time job for more than forty years. Thirty-six of those years I have spent in the college classroom, and nobody writes to full capacity on a full-time teaching job. My life has been public, active, and busy to the point of constant turmoil, tumult, and trauma. Sometimes the only quiet and private place where I could write a sonnet was in the bathroom, because that was the only room where the door could be locked and no one would intrude. I have written mostly at night in my adult life and especially since I have been married, because I was determined not to neglect any members of my family; so I cooked every meal daily, washed dishes and dirty clothes, and nursed sick babies.

I have struggled against dirt and disease as much as I have against sin, which, with my Protestant and Calvinistic background, was always to be abhorred. Every day I have lived, however, I have discovered that the value system with which I was raised is of no value in the society in which I must live. This clash of my ideal with the real, of my dream world with the practical, and the mystical inner life with the sordid and ugly world outside—this clash keeps me on a battlefield, at war, and struggling, even tilting windmills. Always I am determined to overcome adversity, determined to win, determined to be me, myself at my best, always female, always black, and everlastingly free. I think this is always what the woman writer wants to be, herself, inviolate, and whole. Shirley Chisholm, who is also black and female, says she is unbossed and unbought. So am I, and I intend to remain that way. Nobody can tell me what to write because nobody owns me and nobody pulls my strings. I have not been writing to make money or earn my living. I have taught school as my vocation. Writing is my life, but it is an avocation nobody can buy. In this respect I believe I am a free agent, stupid perhaps, but *me* and still free.

When I was younger I considered myself an emancipated woman, freed from the shackles of mind and body that typified the Victorian woman, but never would I call myself the liberated woman in today's vernacular; never the bohemian; never the completely free spirit living in free love; never the lesbian sister; always believing in moderation and nothing to excess; never defying convention, never radical enough to defy tradition; not wanting to be called conservative but never moving beyond the bounds of what I consider the greatest liberty within law, the greatest means of freedom within control. I have lived out my female destiny within the bonds of married love. For me, it could not have been otherwise. In the same way I refuse to judge others, for if tolerance is worth anything, love is worth everything. Everyone should dare to love.

I am therefore fundamentally and contradictorily three things. I am religious almost to the point of orthodoxy—I go to church,

I pray, I believe in the stern dogma and duty of Protestant Christianity; I am radical but I wish to see neither the extreme radical left nor the radical right in control. And I am like the astrological description of a crab, a cancer—quick to retreat into my shell when hurt or attacked. I will wobble around circuitously to find another way out when the way I have chosen has been closed to me. I believe absolutely in the power of my black mind to create, to write, to speak, to witness truth, and to be heard.

Enough for a time about being female and black. What about freedom? The question of freedom is an essential subject for any writer. Without freedom, personal and social, to write as one pleases and to express the will of the people, the writer is in bondage. This bondage may seem to be to others outside oneself but closely related by blood or kinship in some human fashion; or this bondage may appear to be to the inimical forces of the society that so impress or repress that individual.

For the past twenty years or longer I have constantly come into contact with women writers of many different races, classes, nationalities, and degrees. I look back on more than forty years of such associations. Whether at a cocktail party for Muriel Rukeyser at *Poetry* magazine or at Yaddo where Carson Mac-Cullers, Jean Stafford, Karen Blixen, Caroline Slade, and Katherine Anne Porter were guests; or meeting Adrienne Rich and Erica Jong in Massachusetts at Amherst, or having some twenty-five of my black sister-poets at a Phillis Wheatley poetry festival here in Mississippi, including many of the young and brilliant geniuses of this generation; or here in Mississippi where I have come to know Eudora Welty and Ellen Douglas, or having women from foreign countries journey to Jackson to see me, women like Rosey Pool from Amsterdam and a young woman writer a few weeks ago from Turkey or Bessie Head from South Africa—all these experiences have made me know and understand the problems of women writers and our search for freedom.

For the nonwhite woman writer, whether in Africa, Asia, Latin America, the islands of the Caribbean, or the United States, her destiny as a writer has always seemed bleak. Women in Africa and Asia speak of hunger and famine and lack of clean water at the same time that their countries are riddled with warfare. Arab women and Jewish women think of their children in a world that has no hope of peace. Irish women, Protestant and Catholic, speak of the constant threat of bombs and being blown to bits. The women of southern Africa talk of their lives apart from their husbands and their lives in exile from their homelands because of the racial strife in their countries. A Turkish woman speaks of the daily terrorism in her country, of combing the news each evening to see if there are names known on the list of the murdered.

I have read the works of scores of these women. I saw Zora Neale Hurston when I was a child and I know what a hard life she had. I read the works of a dozen black women in the Harlem Renaissance, who despite their genius received only a small success. Langston Hughes translated Gabriela Mistral, and I read her before she won the Nobel Prize for Literature. Hualing Nieh Engle tells of her native China, and my friends in Mexico speak of the unbelievable poverty of their people. Each of these internationally known women writers is my sister in search of an island of freedom. Each is part of me and I am part of her.

Writing is a singularly individual matter. At least it has historically been so. Only the creative, original individual working alone has been considered the artist working with the fire of imagination. Today, this appears no longer to be the case. In America, our affluent, electronic, and materialistic society does not respect the imaginative writer regardless of sex, race, color, or creed. It never thought highly of the female worker, whether an Emily Dickinson or Amy Lowell, Phillis Wheatley, or Ellen Glasgow. Our American society has no respect for the literary values of intellectual honesty nor for originality and creativity in the sensitive individual. Books today are managed, being written by a committee and promoted by the conglomerate, corporate structures. Best sellers are designed as commodities to sell in the marketplace before a single word is written. Plastic people who are phony writers pretending to take us into a more humanistic century are quickly designated the paper heroes who are promoted with super-HYPE. Do I sound bitter? A Black Woman

Writer who is free? Free to do what? To publish? To be promoted? Of what value is freedom in a money-mad society? What does freedom mean to the racially biased and those bigots who have deep religious prejudices? What is my hope as a woman writer?

I am a black woman living in a male-oriented and male-dominated white world. Moreover, I live in an American Empire where the financial tentacles of the American Octopus in the business-banking world extend around the globe, with the multinationals and international conglomerates encircling everybody and impinging on the lives of every single soul. What then are my problems? They are the pressures of a sexist, racist, violent, and most materalistic society. In such a society life is cheap and expendable; honor is a rag to be scorned; and justice is violated. Vice and money control business, the judicial system, government, sports, entertainment, publishing, education, and the church. Every other arm of this hydra-headed monster must render lip service and yeoman support to extend, uphold, and perpetuate the syndicated world-system. The entire world of the press, whether broadcast or print journalism, must acquiesce and render service or be eliminated. And what have I to do with this? How do I operate? How long can I live under fear before I too am blown to bits and must crumble into anonymous dust and nonentity?

Now I am sixty-three. I wish I could live the years all over. I am sure I would make the same mistakes and do all the things again exactly the same way. But perhaps I might succeed a little more; and wistfully I hope, too, I might have written more books.

What are the critical decisions I must make as a woman, as a, writer? They are questions of compromise, and of guilt. They are the answers to the meaning and purpose of all life; questions of the value of life lived half in fear and half in faith, cringing under the whip of tyranny or dying, too, for what one dares to believe and dying with dignity and without fear. I must believe there is more wisdom in a righteous path that leads to death than an ignominious path of living shame; that the writer is still in the avant-garde for Truth and Justice, for Freedom, Peace, and

Human Dignity. I must believe that women are still in that humanistic tradition and I must cast my lot with them.

Across the world humanity seems in ferment, in war, fighting over land and the control of people's lives; people who are hungry, sick, and suffering, most of all fearful. The traditional and historic role of womankind is ever the role of the healing and annealing hand, whether the outworn modes of nurse, and mother, cook, and sweetheart. As a writer these are still her concerns. These are still the stuff about which she writes, the human condition, the human potential, the human destiny. Her place, let us be reminded, is anywhere she chooses to be, doing what she has to do, creating, healing, and always being herself. Female, Black, and Free, this is what I always want to be.

DIANE JOHNSON

ASPIRADORA

A s women we are taught not to speak of ourselves, but of the other person, asking him "What do you do? Tell me about your work." One's own work becomes almost a secret and antisocial pursuit, a hobby or eccentricity, like button collecting, or dypsomania. At least it has taken me some years to learn to speak of my own work, especially in a magisterial tone, as something that might be of interest to others.

The subject here I take to be: how I do my work, and how I think about it. But the odd thing is that because I am not used to speaking of it, I'm not used to thinking about it either. The time I have for it, I spend doing it. What I think about is the work at hand, the novel or essay, trying to get the thoughts right, putting the events in the right order, and the names of the characters. In other words, a writing day is so filled with practical decisions that one tends to lose sight of, or never to have glimpsed, "My Work" in the overall sense—the things that characterize it, and distinguish it from the work of other people.

I am always interested, though, to read critics who have views on my typical themes or techniques, and I can usually see what they mean, one exception being violence. I know that critics often think of me as being preoccupied with violence, whereas to me it seems I never think of it at all. In the books there are violent episodes, no doubt about it. But I think of these as being reflections of life in our society—social realism, not my psyche in particular.

How I think about my work is indistinguishable from the way I think about my needlepoint or cooking: here is the project I'm involved in. It is play. In this sense, all my life is spent in play—sewing or needlepoint, or picking flowers, or writing, or buying groceries. Being a housewife and mother, I have duties, too, but I am apt to shirk duty or wander off in the middle of it, so I can't really claim to have sacrificed my writing to my housework, the way it seems to some women that they have done.

I tend to get interested in technical or formal problems in novel-writing, and I think each of my books reflects a slightly different preoccupation, which makes each differ from the last. I think that to set oneself new problems is the only way to grow as a writer; but I know that readers, on the other hand, tend to wish you would do the same things over (until you get them right, anyhow). I suppose, at first, a writer's preoccupation tends to be with point of view, since you quickly learn that this is the most crucial and difficult choice you as the author have to make. My first novel, *Fair Game*—which is totally out of print, I hardly have any copies myself and it has been years since I looked at it—was written from the points of view of several male characters who were all in love with one female character, Dabney. joking back on it, I find it strange that I would try to write from a male point of view, let alone three or four, and even stranger that I should have avoided the consciousness of the woman character. In a way this was part of the novel's design—the point being that none of them understood her and only saw her as the mirror of their desires, each differently. But now I wonder, too, whether I wasn't influenced (this was around 1965) by all the traditional novels I had read, which usually have male narrators, and hence found the male voice easier to emulate. Growing up, I didn't like girl's novels—hated *Little Women*. I liked sea stories, of pirates and adventure. At that period female narrators tended to be mad, or desperately subjective, full of love or fear or some other emotion, and not employed for the purpose of rendering objective and reliable accounts of the world.

I became aware of this tradition of the unreliable female narrator when writing *The Shadow Knows*, or rather when reading the reviews of it. At that time, I was interested in the detective genre, at least in its smart, French incarnations, and the design of *Shadow* shows this—there's a detective ("the famous inspector") and a suspense situation. Someone is trying to murder the heroine, there are suspects and so on. It seemed to me that the metaphorical possibilities of detective stories for getting at issues of urban fear, guilt, and race relations in American society are enormous, and these were for me the subject of this novel. These were serious preoccupations for me, so of course I was quite surprised to read a number of critics who understood the novel as being about paranoia, a woman close to madness, the thinness of the line between madness and sanity and so on. In other words, many readers were not able to believe objective descriptions of events ("someone has put a dead cat on my door-step") because (I suppose) the narrator was a woman.

Thinking about this later, I have come to see that the fact that the woman was young and, as people say nowadays, sexually active made people believe her less—the problem that rape victims have. An elderly grandmother can be used as a reliable narrator. But I also have to admit, speaking again of the critical reception of *The Shadow Knows*, that critics often see things in a novel that the writer wasn't conscious of putting in, and often one can see that the critics are right. In this case, though, I never have quite understood why people can have thought that the sensible N. was near to madness.

People complained, too, about the end of that novel, when she is raped by a stranger in the garage, and finds herself somehow in harmony with this event, or relieved by it. What I had in mind was ending with her in the state of mind when everything bad that can happen has happened, leaving her free of further dread. But alas, some people took me to be saying that women like to be raped. I think now I would have to choose some other, less politically significant act of violence to make the point.

I had in mind that the rapist was the Famous Inspector, but the editor at Knopf convinced me that that was "too much," so I left the matter unresolved. I believe I have a tendency to go too far with endings, and someone always talks me out of the last little sting in the tail I had planned. In *Persian Nights*, when the heroine, Chloe Fowler, finally gets on a plane to go home, I had a sentence which would make you realize she had got on the wrong plane (there being great chaos in the Tehran airport) and was going to end up in Geneva. Of course this wouldn't have changed anything—she would have just gotten back to the United States a little later, with some inconvenience—it wasn't really important at all. So I acceded to editorial inquietude and took it out.

I think I have been too docile about titles. I forget what I planned to call *Fair Game*, but it wasn't that. My next novel, *Loving Hands at Home*, I had planned to call *Being Alma*, after a character that has a kind of inspirational significance to the heroine, Karen. Alma was the bad girl in her hometown, the one who found out about sex and economic realities before anybody else. *Loving Hands* was an early version of a novel that many women writers have written since— the bored or disappointed housewife novel. A particular favorite of mine in this genre is Sheila Ballantine's *Norma Jean the Termite Queen*—not a title that does justice to this wonderfully witty and trenchant novel. Another title of my own that I was made to change was *Aspiradora*. This became *Lying Low*, which I think is a pretty good title too, but I will always think of the novel as *Aspiradora*. This word, with its reverberations of "aspirations" and its specific meaning, vacuum cleaner, refers to one of the central characters, the Brazilian Ouida, who is the cleaning lady and admirer of American manners.

It was with this novel, *Lying Low*, that I finally stopped feeling the ghost of Henry James glaring over my shoulder in disapproval at the mélange of points of view I find myself using, and became comfortable suiting myself in this matter. I know what James said, of course, and deeply revere his strictures on most things. I almost love his prefaces better than his novels. Almost no other writer has left so many directions and interesting observations about the art of novel-writing. I also love Ford Madox Ford's manifesto, in his biography of Conrad. I came under the spell of Ford's *The Good Soldier* when I was writing *The Shadow Knows*. This elusive novel of passion and menace is so artfully constructed that I took a week and outlined it, according to a complicated system of notation I devised, not merely noting what happened but isolating the themes, the points of climax, the chronology, and so on. This was so helpful to me in understanding structure that I then outlined *The Shadow*, and later, *Lying Low*. In between writing these two books, I worked with Stanley Kubrick, the director, on the screenplay of his film *The Shining*. Here, too, we worked very hard on the outline before ever writing any of the scenes, and this left me convinced that outlines (not hard, inflexible, calculating ones) are indispensable, if one has the patience to do them, as a means of perfecting the structure, and of understanding a lot about a novel before plunging in and making mistakes by rushing ahead, the way one does with one's first novel, innocent of all the formal decisions that will have to be made.

I became wary of speaking of the outline, for instance to a workshop of creative-writing students, because it seems to be in many minds a kind of commercial gimmick, something you are told to do in "how-to" books, or by agents or publishers who tell you to submit three chapters and an outline. No one would understand my outlines—they don't tell any of the events or even, often, the subject, and they look like this:

CcDccQ R s'1

In a new novel, one I've just finished, called *Health and Happiness* (as yet no one has suggested I change the title), I got interested in the problem of, or task of, trying to write a true comedy of manners. Thus the issues became tone and pace (in addition, of course, to characters, point of view, and what actually happens). The subject is indicated in the title, the connection between health and happiness, worked out in a hospital setting. This setting, I found, was fraught with pitfalls, mainly the difficulty of avoiding melodrama, for hospitals are implicitly melodramatic, full of death, pain, and crisis. When a novel isn't yet published (at which time I can forget about it), I am still in the disappointed frame of mind in which the writer, faced with what she has wrought, can't help but compare it to what she had in mind. Inevitably the novel you end up with is different than the ideal composition you were planning—I wanted mine to be sprightly, very sharp about doctors and their foibles and the medical profession in general, and women—their wives, nurses, and so on. Susan Cheever has a novel whose title I greatly wanted for my own: *Doctors and Women*. I am sure our two novels are nothing alike, but I haven't dared to read hers, in case of some similarity which would have made me start mine over!

I became aware in writing *Health and Happiness* that I was touching on matters I explored in the early novel I haven't yet mentioned, *Burning*, which I also thought of as being a novel of manners, and of place, Los Angeles. It takes place in one day, the day of a fire, one of those richly metaphorical fires they are always having in Los Angeles which consume the houses of rich people and so on. I've always been fond of this novel—more than other people were, I have to admit. It did teach me, though, that it is unwise to write about Los Angeles, or to set things there, if you want people in other parts of the country to believe that the events and conditions you are describing have any general relevance. Having lived there, I myself have a great affection for Los Angeles novels—Alison Lurie's wonderful *Nowhere City*, and all the novels of Carolyn See, for example.

Besides novels, I've written various essays and two biographies. People often ask which I prefer, and whether I find it hard to write both nonfiction and fiction. The answer to the latter is no. I enjoy writing essays, I suppose because I am an opinionated person and it is a great luxury to be enabled to express these opinions and preach a little in a form more concise than the concealed didacticism that is (always, anybody's) novel.

Biographies are another matter. I liked writing *Lesser Lives*, the story of a circle of minor Victorian figures, at the center of which was a woman, Mary Ellen Meredith, the daughter of Thomas Love Peacock, wife of George Meredith, and lover of Henry Wallis, a minor pre-Raphaelite. The premise was that minor figures have lives which seem important to them if not to history. The fun of writing this book was that I had only the tiniest traces of research, little packets of letters that no one had ever read before, some wills, and a tattered pink parasol. It was a work of imaginative sympathy, I suppose. In the case of Dashiell Hammett, my other biographical subject, I experienced a problem common with biographers, a failure of imaginative sympathy. I would find myself becoming censorious over his alcoholism, the waste of his talent, his tendencies to beat up women and skip out on his hotel bills, and would have to talk myself into remembering the gallant things about his response to his sad life. With Hammett, I let him speak for himself (by quoting abundantly from his letters) and made very few attempts at interpretation myself.

Because certain questions are always asked after a reading—How, with what, do you write? How do you think up your subjects?—I assume these are interesting questions. I know that writers are interested in such matters, and among ourselves will discuss word processors and such. I remember getting a letter years ago, before such machines, from Alison Lurie, which said "a typewriter ribbon can be revived, in an emergency, by soaking it in vegetable oil. Pass it on." Now I write in longhand or on a little electronic typewriter, a portable light gadget. I have three of them—one at my home in San Francisco, one in a little writing room I rent, and one in Paris where I have an apartment. I write on yellow paper—I don't know why that seems important. I have a friend who writes on pink or blue paper—I never could do that. Blue! A color I particularly detest.

Some writers start from a character or even a title, or something glimpsed by accident, as Henry James describes doing. But I start from an idea, a sort of thematic notion. I might think of it as A Novel about Americans Abroad in the Third World—this became *Persian Nights*. I have mentioned how I thought of *The Shadow Knows. Lying Low* was to be about the issues of involvement and commitment. *Health and Happiness*, as I have said, about modern medicine. All these are political themes, and in my own mind I am kind of a political novelist. I am always surprised when critics find a tone of tragedy or romance, though it is fair to say that I try for all these things at once, for I believe that a novel can be funny and serious at once, and should be. All the writers I admire are funny and serious—Waugh and Kalka, Austen and Dickens, to speak of the classics. The greatest writers have all been funny. I suppose a writer doesn't have to choose a category, but you do find yourself put into one by others after the fact, and I guess mine is a sort of serio-comic satiric category. That is fine with me, but I hope it doesn't mean that my work isn't taken seriously, for it is seriously meant.

My impression is that, though different writers find the genesis of a novel in different ways, all are alike in their sense of having the work inside them in some potential form. The analogy to gestation is very exact. The work must be born to be known. One's sense of it beforehand is strong, yet so subvocal, so unconscious, and often so different from what the reader will find it to be about that the possibilities of misunderstanding, between the writer and the work, and between the writer and the reader, are very great indeed.

Because the process of writing *Health and Happiness* is fresh in my mind, I can recapitulate something of my thinking at the beginning. I knew I wanted to write about doctors. What about them? Well, the relationship of doctors and nurses, doctors and patients—doctors and women. The erotic power and the power of fear that they have over others. The complexities of their job (I am married to a doctor). Something of the situation of modern medicine, its moral situation.

Once you think of all the things a novel is to be about, you still have to embody it in a story. Between these two steps, a great painful chasm, a gap, a silence can prevail, at least for me. As in darkness, I grope toward the story, something to hang the aboutness on. I think the process is opposite for some writers—they think of a gripping story first, and then the complexities and moral ramifications develop as they write.

In *Health and Happiness* I hit upon using an experience of my own, one day when I woke up and noticed that one of my arms was swollen up. From here it was easy to find a heroine to whom this is to happen. But, if she is the patient, she won't be able to see and know a lot of things around the hospital—someone else will be needed. For this, I found Mimi Franklin, the coordinator of volunteer services. And what is a doctor novel without a doctor hero? Here I invent Philip Watts, the head doctor. In this way, little by little, the characters assemble on the stage. I change their names a dozen times. Eventually they tell me which is their real name. Almost all novelists testify to the curious experience of having characters refuse to do what you want them to, and change the course of a novel. This has often happened to me. Mimi, the volunteer coordinator, remained mysterious to me until a friend pointed out that she was exceptionally tall, and that accounted for her shyness and reserve. That helped me to realize other things about her. In this novel, Philip, the main male character, seemed to see things most closely to the way I would see them, though normally I feel this affinity more for the female characters. Of course the writer is really all the characters, not just the Emma Bovary character.

People sometimes ask about, or assume, feminism in my works. I in turn assume that any nice woman is a feminist in some sense. I don't set out to explicate feminist themes in my work though, and I object to things that concern half the human race (all the human race really) being relegated to the status of political issue instead of being seen as an aspect of human experience, of concern and interest to everybody. If you are a woman writer, you will naturally see things from a female perspective, your experience having been shaped in that way, and that inclines you to views which other people often think are "political" when they are merely literal.

I have always found this odd. For instance, because women tend to have a satirical view of men, and you are writing a scene in which women talk about men, and you put down what real women would say, people imagine it is you satirizing men. To be fair, I believe that the same thing happens to male authors—a notable example being Leonard Michaels's *The Men's Club*, in which the author, meaning to expose the crudity and poverty of some men's emotional lives, was accused of himself holding the sexist views his characters held.

I suppose that the moral views and emotional state of the author are always a kind of subtext in reading a novel. Because the writer is hiding behind a construction, the reader feels impelled to try to spy her out, a situation different from what happens in poetry, or in the estay, where the writer tries to explain her views as clearly as she can—but to begin to discourse on the general, instead of the particulars of my work, is, I think, a sign to myself that I have said as much as I can.

NATALIA GINZBURG

MY VOCATION

MY vocation is to write and I have known this for a long time. I hope I won't be misunderstood; I know nothing about the value of the things I am able to write. I know that writing is my vocation. When I sit down to write I feel extraordinarily at ease, and I move in an element which, it seems to me, I know extraordinarily well; I use tools that are familiar to me and they fit snugly in my hands. If I do something else, if I study a foreign language or try to learn history or geography or shorthand or if I try and speak in public or take up knitting or go on a journey, I suffer and constantly ask myself how others do these things: it always seems to me that there must be some correct way of doing these things which others know about and I don't. And it seems to me that I am deaf and blind and I feel a sort of sickness in the pit of my stomach. But when I write I never imagine that there is perhaps a better way of writing which other writers follow. I am not interested in what other writers do. But here I had better make it plain that I can only write stories. If I try to write a critical essay or an article that has been commissioned for a newspaper I don't do it very well. I have to search laboriously, as if it were outside myself, for what I am writing now. I can do it a little better than I can learn a foreign language or speak in public, but only a little better. And I always feel that I am cheating the reader with words that I have borrowed or filched from various places. I suffer and feel that I am in exile. But when I write stories I am like someone who is in her own country, walking along streets that she has known since she was a child, between walls and trees that are hers. My vocation is to write stories—invented things or things which I can remember from my own life, but in any case stories, things that are

concerned only with memory and imagination and have nothing
to do with erudition. This is my vocation and I shall work at it till
I die. I am very happy with my vocation and I would not change
it for anything in the world. I realized that it was my vocation a
long time ago. Between the ages of five and ten I was still unsure,
and sometimes I imagined that I would be a painter, sometimes
that I would ride out on horseback and conquer countries,
sometimes that I would invent new machines that would be very
important. But I have known since I was ten, and I worked as
hard as I could at poems and novels. I still have those poems. The
first poems are clumsy and they have errors of versification in
them, but they are quite pleasant; and then, little by little, as time
passed I wrote poems that became less and less clumsy but more
and more boring and silly. However, I didn't know this and I was
ashamed of the clumsy poems, while those that were silly and
not so clumsy seemed to me to be very beautiful, and I used to
think that one day some famous poet would discover them and
have them published and write long articles about me; I
imagined the words and phrases of those articles and I
composed them, from beginning to end, in my head. I imagined
that I would win the Fracchia Prize. I had heard that there was
such a prize for writers. As I was unable to publish my poems in a
book, since I didn't know any famous poets, I copied them neatly
into an exercise book and drew a little flower on the title page
and made an index and everything. It became very easy for me to
write poems. I wrote about one a day. I realized that if I didn't
want to write it was enough for me to read some poems by
Pascoli or Gozzano or Corazzini and then I immediately wanted
to. My poems came out as imitation Pascoli or imitation Gozzano
or imitation Corazzini and then finally very imitation D'Annunzio
when I found out that he also existed. However, I never thought
that I would write poetry all my life. I wanted to write novels
sooner or later. I wrote three or four during those years. There
was one called *Marion or the Gipsy Girl*, another called *Molly
and Dolly* (a humorous detective story), another called *A
Woman* (à La D'Annunzio; in the second person; the story of a
woman abandoned by her husband; I remember that there was
also a cook who was a Negress), and then one that was very long

and complicated with terrible stories of kidnapped girls and
carriages so that I was too afraid to write it when I was alone in
the house: I can remember nothing about it except that there
was one phrase which pleased me very much and that tears
came into my eyes as I wrote it, "He said: 'Ah! Isabella is
leaving.'" The chapter finished with this phrase which was very
important because it was said by the man who loved Isabella
although he did not know this as he had not yet confessed it to
himself. I don't remember anything about this man (I think he
had a reddish beard). Isabella had long black hair with blue
highlights in it; I don't know anything else about her. I know that
for a long time I would feel a shiver of joy whenever I said "Ah!
Isabella is leaving" to myself. I also often used to repeat a phrase
which I found in a serialized novel in *Stampa* which went like
this, "Murderer of Gilonne, where have you put my child?" But I
was not as sure about my novels as I was about the poems. When
I reread them I always discovered a weakness somewhere or
other, something wrong which spoiled everything and which
was impossible to change. I always used to muddle up the past
and the present; I was unable to fix the story in a particular time.
Parts of it were convents and carriages and a general feeling of
the French Revolution, and parts of it were policemen with
truncheons; and then all of a sudden there would be a little gray
housewife with a sewing machine and cats as in Carola Prosperi's
novels, and this didn't go very well with the carriages and
convents. I wavered between Carola Prosperi and Victor Hugo
and Nick Carter's stories; I didn't really know what I wanted to
do. I was also very keen on Annie Vivanti. There is a phrase in
The Devourers when she is writing to a stranger and says to him,
"I dress in brown." This was another phrase which for a long
time I repeated to myself. During the day. I used to murmur to
myself these phrases which gave me so much pleasure—
"Murderer of Gilonne," "Isabella is leaving," "I dress in
brown"—and I felt immensely happy.

Writing poetry was easy. I was very pleased with my poems; to
me they seemed almost perfect. I could not see what difference
there was between them and real, published poems by real
poets. I could not see why when I gave them to my brothers to

read they laughed and said I would have done better to study Greek. I thought that perhaps my brothers didn't know much about poetry. Meanwhile I had to go to school and study Greek, Latin, mathematics, history—and I suffered a good deal and felt that I was in exile. I spent my days writing poems and copying them out in exercise books; I did not study for my lessons so I used to set the alarm for five in the morning. The alarm went off but I went on sleeping. I woke at seven, when there was no longer any time to study and I had to dress to go to school. I was not happy, I was always extremely afraid and filled with feelings of guilt and confusion. When I got to school I studied history during the Latin lesson, Greek during the history lesson, and so on, and I learnt nothing. For quite a while I thought it was all worth it because my poems were so beautiful, but at a certain moment I began to think that perhaps they were not so beautiful and it became tedious for me to write them and take the trouble to find subjects; it seemed to me that I had already dealt with every possible subject, and used all the possible words and rhymes—*speranza, lontananza; pensiero, mistero; vento, argento; fragranza, speranza* (hope, distance; thought, mystery; wind, silver; fragrance, hope). I couldn't find anything else to say. Then a very nasty period began for me, and I spent afternoons playing about with words that no longer gave me any pleasure while at the same time I felt guilty and ashamed about school. It never entered my head that I had mistaken my vocation—I wanted to write as much as ever, it was just that I could not understand why my days had suddenly become so barren and empty of words.

The first serious piece I wrote was a story, a short story of five or six pages; it came from me like a miracle in a single evening, and when afterwards I went to bed I was tired, bewildered, worn out. I had the feeling that it was a serious piece, the first that I had ever written: the poems and the novels about girls and carriages suddenly seemed very far away from me; they were the naïve and ridiculous creatures of another age and they belonged to a time that had disappeared for good. There were characters in this new story. Isabella and the man with the reddish beard were not characters; I didn't know anything about them beyond

the words and phrases with which I described them—they
appeared as if at random and not by my design. I had chosen the
words and phrases I used for them by chance; it was as if I had a
sack and had indiscriminately pulled out of it now a beard and
now a cook who was a Negress or some other usable item. But
this time it was not a game. This time I had invented characters
with names that I could not possibly have changed; I could not
have changed any part of them and I knew a great deal about
them—I knew how their lives had been up to the day of my story
even though I did not talk about this in the story as it was not
necessary. And I knew all about the house, the bridge, the moon,
and the river. I was seventeen and I had failed in Latin, Greek,
and mathematics. I had cried a lot when I found out. But now
that I had written the story I felt a little less ashamed. It was
summer, a summer night. A window that gave on to the garden
was open and dark moths fluttered about the lamp. I had written
my story on squared paper and I felt happy as never before in my
life; I felt I had a wealth of thoughts and words within me. The
man was called Maurizio, the woman was called Anna, and the
child was called Villi, and the bridge, the moon, and the river
were also there. These things existed in me. And the man and the
woman were neither good nor evil, but funny and a little sad and
it seemed to me that I had discovered how people in books
should be—funny and at the same time sad. Whichever way I
looked at this story it seemed beautiful to me: there were no
mistakes in it; everything happened as it should, at the right time.
At that moment it seemed to me that I could write millions of
stories.

   And in fact I wrote quite a few, at intervals of a month or
two—some were quite good and some not so good. Now I
discovered that it is tiring to write something seriously. It is a
bad sign if it doesn't make you tired. You cannot hope to write
something serious frivolously flitting hither and thither, as it
were, with one hand tied behind your back. You cannot get off
so lightly. When someone writes something seriously he is lost
in it, he is sucked down into it up to his eyebrows; and if there is
a very strong emotion that is preoccupying him, if he is very
happy or very unhappy for some let us say mundane reason

which has nothing to do with the piece he is writing, then if what he is writing is real and deserves to live all those other feelings will become dormant in him. He cannot hope to keep his dear happiness or dear unhappiness whole and fresh before him; everything goes off into the distance and vanishes and he is left alone with his page. No happiness or unhappiness that is not strictly relevant to that page can exist in him; he cannot possess or belong to anything else—and if it does not happen like this, well that is a sign that the page is worthless.

And so for a certain period—which lasted about six years—I wrote short stories. Since I had discovered that characters existed it seemed to me that to *have* a character was enough to make a story. So I was always hunting for characters; I looked at the people in the tram and on the street and when I found a face that seemed suitable for a story I wove some moral details and a little anecdote around it. I also went hunting for details of dress and people's appearance, and how their houses looked inside; if I went into a new room I tried to describe it silently to myself and I tried to find some small detail which would fit well in a story. I kept a notebook in which I wrote down some of the details I had discovered, or little similes, or episodes which I promised myself I would use in stories. For example, I would write in my notebook "She came out of the bathroom trailing the cord of her dressing-gown behind her like a long tail," "How the lavatory stinks in this house—the child said to him—When I go, I hold my breath—he added sadly," "His curls like bunches of grapes," "Red and black blankets on an unmade bed," "A pale face like a peeled potato." But I discovered how difficult it was to use these phrases when I was writing a story. The notebook became a kind of museum of phrases that were crystallized and embalmed and very difficult to use. I tried endlessly to slip the red and black blankets or the curls like bunches of grapes into a story but I never managed to. So the notebook was no help to me. I realized that in this vocation there is no such thing as "Savings." If someone thinks, That's a fine detail and I don't want to waste it in the story I'm writing at the moment, I've plenty of good material here, I'll keep it in reserve for another story I'm going to write, that detail will crystallize inside him and he won't be able to use it. When someone writes a story he should throw the best of everything into it, the best of whatever he possesses and has seen, all the best things that he has accumulated throughout his life. If you carry details around inside yourself for a long time without making use of them, they wear out and waste away. Not only details but everything, all your ideas and clever notions. At the time when I was writing short stories made up of characters I had chanced on, and minute descriptive details, at that time I once saw a handcart being pushed through the street and on it was a huge mirror in a gilded frame. The greenish evening sky was reflected in it and as I stopped to watch while it went past I was feeling extremely happy, and I had the impression that something important had happened. I had been feeling very happy even before I saw the mirror, and it suddenly seemed to me that in the greenish resplendent mirror with its gilded frame the image of my own happiness was passing by me. For a long time I thought that I would put this in a story; for a long time simply remembering that handcart with the mirror on top of it made me want to write. But I was never able to include it anywhere and finally I realized that the image had died in me. Nevertheless it was very important. Because at the time when I was writing my short stories I always concentrated on gray, squalid people and things, I sought out a contemptible kind of reality lacking in glory. There was a certain malignancy in the taste I had at that time for finding minute details, an avid, mean desire for little things—little as fleas are little; I was engaged in an obstinate, scandal-mongering hunt for fleas. The mirror on the handcart seemed to offer me new possibilities, perhaps the ability to look at a more glorious and splendid kind of reality which did not require minute descriptions and cleverly noticed details but which could be conveyed in one resplendent, felicitous image.

In the last analysis I despised the characters in the short stories I was writing at that time. Since I had discovered that it works well if a character is sad and comic I made characters who, because of their comic and pitiable qualities, were so contemptible and lacking in glory that I myself could not love them. My characters always had some nervous tic or obsession or physical deformity, or some rather ridiculous bad habit—they had a broken arm in a black sling, or they had sties in their eyes, or they stuttered, or they scratched their buttocks as they talked, or they limped a little. I always had to characterize them in some such way. For me this was a method of running away from my fear that they would turn out too vague, a way of capturing their humanity (which, subconsciously, I did not believe in). Because at that time I did not realize—though when I saw the mirror on the handcart I began, confusedly, to realize it—that I was no longer dealing with characters but with puppets, quite well painted and resembling men, but puppets. When I invented them I immediately characterized them, I marked them with some grotesque detail, and there was something nasty in this; I had a kind of malign resentment against reality. It was not a resentment based on anything real, because at that time I was a happy girl, but it appeared as a kind of reaction against naïveté; it was that special resentment with which a naïve person who always thinks she is being made a fool of defends herself—the resentment of a peasant who finds himself in a city for a while and sees thieves everywhere. At first I was bold, because this seemed to me to be a great ironic triumph over the naïvely pathetic effusions which were all too apparent in my poems. Irony and nastiness seemed to be very important weapons in my hands; I thought they would help me write like a man, because at that time I wanted terribly to write like a man and I had a horror of anyone realizing from what I wrote that I was a woman. I almost always invented male characters because they would be the furthest and most separate from myself.

I became reasonably good at blocking out a story, at getting rid of superfluous material and introducing details and conversations at the appropriate moments. I wrote dry, clear stories that contained no blunders or mistakes of tone and that came to a convincing conclusion. But after a while I had had enough of this. The faces of people in the street no longer said anything interesting to me. Someone had a sty and someone had his cap on back to front and someone was wearing a scarf instead of a shirt, but these things no longer mattered to me. I was fed up with looking at things and people and describing them to myself.

The world became silent for me. I could no longer find words to describe it, I no longer had any words capable of giving me pleasure. I didn't have anything anymore. I tried to remember the mirror, but even that had died in me. I carried a burden of embalmed objects around inside of me—silent faces and ashen words, places and voices and gestures that were a dead weight on my heart, that had no flicker of life in them. And then my children were born and when they were very little I could not understand how anyone could sit herself down to write if she had children. I did not see how I could separate myself from them in order to follow someone or other's fortunes in a story. I began to feel contempt for my vocation. Now and again I longed for it desperately and felt that I was in exile, but I tried to despise it and make fun of it and occupy myself solely with the children. I believed I had to do this. I spent my time on creamed rice and creamed barley and wondering whether there was sun or not or wind or not so that I could take the children out for a walk. The children seemed extremely important to me because they were a way of leaving my stupid stories and stupid embalmed characters behind. But I felt a ferocious longing within me and sometimes at night I almost wept when I remembered how beautiful my vocation was. I thought that I would recover it some day or other but I did not know when: I thought that I would have to wait till my children grew up and left me. Because the feeling I then had for my children was one that I had not yet learnt to control. But then little by little I learnt, and it did not even take that long. I still made tomato sauce and semolina, but simultaneously I thought about what I could be writing. At that time we were living in very beautiful countryside, in the south. I remembered my own city's streets and hills, and those streets and hills mingled with the streets and hills and meadows of the place where we were, and a new nature, something that I was once again able to love, appeared. I felt homesick for my city and in retrospect I loved it very much. I loved and understood it in a way that I had never done when I lived there, and I also loved the place where we were then living—a countryside that was white and dusty in the southern sunlight; wide meadows of scorched, bristling grass stretched away from my window, and a memory of the avenues and plane-trees and high houses of my city assailed me; all this slowly took fire in me and I had a very strong desire to write. I wrote a long story, the longest I had ever written. I started writing again like someone who has never written, because it was a long time since I had written anything, and the words seemed rinsed and fresh; everything was new and, as it were, untouched, and full of taste and fragrance. I wrote in the afternoons while a local girl took my children out for a walk, and I wrote greedily and joyfully; it was a beautiful autumn and I felt very happy every day. I put a few invented people into my story and a few real people from the countryside where we were living; and some of the words that came to me as I was writing were idioms and imprecations local to that area, and which I had not known before, and these new expressions were like a yeast that fermented and gave life to all the old words. The main character was a woman, but very different from myself. Now I no longer wanted to write like a man, because I had had children and I thought I knew a great many things about tomato sauce and even if I didn't put them into my story it helped my vocation. It seemed to me that women knew things about their children that a man could never know. I wrote my story very quickly, as if I were afraid that it would run away. I called it a novel, but perhaps it was not a novel. But up till then I had always written very quickly, and always very short things, and at a certain moment I thought I realized why. Because I had brothers who were much older than me and when I was small if I talked at table they always told me to be quiet. And so I was used to speaking very fast, in a headlong fashion with the smallest possible number of words, and always afraid that the others would start talking among themselves again and stop listening to me. Perhaps this seems a rather stupid explanation; nevertheless that is how it was.

I said that the time when I was writing what I called a novel was a very happy time for me. Nothing serious had ever happened in my life; I knew nothing about sickness or betrayal or loneliness or death. Nothing in my life had ever fallen to pieces, except futile things; nothing dear to my heart had ever been snatched away from me. I had only suffered from the listless melancholy of adolescence and the pain of not knowing how to write. And so I was happy in a fulfilled, calm way, without fear or anxiety, and with a complete faith in the stability and durability of earthly happiness. When we are happy we feel that we are cooler, clearer, more separate from reality. When we are happy we tend to create characters who are very different from ourselves; we see them in a cold, clear light as things separate from us. While our imagination and inventive energy work assertively within us we avert our eyes from our own happy, contented state and pitilessly—with a free, cruel, ironic, proud gaze—fix them on other beings. It is easy for us to invent characters, many characters, who are fundamentally different from us, and it is easy for us to construct our stories solidly— they are, as it were, well-drained and stand in a cold, clear light. What we then lack, when we are happy in this special way that has no tears or anxiety or fear in it, what we then lack is any tender, intimate sympathy with our characters and with the places and things we write about. What we lack is compassion. Superficially we are much more generous in the sense that we always find the strength to be interested in others and devote our time to them—we are not that preoccupied with ourselves because we don't need anything. But this interest of ours in others, which is so lacking in tenderness, can only get at a few relatively external aspects of their characters. The world has only one dimension for us and lacks secrets and shadows; we are able to guess at and create the sadness we have not experienced by virtue of the imaginative strength within us, but we always see it in a sterile, frozen light as something that does not concern us and that has no roots within us.

Our personal happiness or unhappiness, our *terrestrial* condition, has a great importance for the things we write. I said before that at the moment someone is writing he is miraculously driven to forget the immediate circumstances of his own life. This is certainly true. But whether we are happy or unhappy leads us to write in one way or another. When we are happy our imagination is stronger; when we are unhappy our memory works with greater vitality. Suffering makes the imagination weak and lazy; it moves, but unwillingly and heavily, with the weak movements of someone who is ill, with the weariness and caution of sick, feverish limbs; it is difficult for us to turn our eyes away from our own life and our own state, from the thirst and restlessness that pervade us. And so memories of our own past constantly crop up in the things we write; our own voice constantly echoes there and we are unable to silence it. A particular sympathy grows up between us and the characters that we invent—a sympathy that is tender and almost maternal, warm and damp with tears, intimately physical and stifling. We are deeply, painfully rooted in every being and thing in the world, the world which has become filled with echoes and trembling and shadows, to which we are bound by a devout and passionate pity. Then we risk foundering on a dark lake of stagnant, dead water, and dragging our mind's creations down with us, so that they are left to perish among dead rats and rotting flowers in a dark, warm whirlpool. As far as the things we write are concerned, there is a danger in grief just as there is a danger in happiness. Because poetic beauty is a mixture of ruthlessness, pride, irony, physical tenderness, of imagination and memory, of clarity and obscurity—and if we cannot gather all things together we are left with something meager, unreliable, and hardly alive.

And you have to realize that you cannot hope to console yourself for your grief by writing. You cannot deceive yourself by hoping for caresses and lullabies from your vocation. In my life there have been interminable, desolate, empty Sundays in which I desperately wanted to write something that would console me for my loneliness and boredom, so that I could be calmed and soothed by phrases and words. But I could not write a single line. My vocation has always rejected me; it does not want to know about me. Because this vocation is never a consolation or a way of passing the time. It is not a companion. This vocation is a master who is able to beat us till the blood flows, a master who reviles and condemns us. We must swallow our saliva and our tears and grit our teeth and dry the blood from our wounds and serve him. Serve him when he asks. Then he will help us up onto our feet, fix our feet firmly on the ground; he will help us overcome madness and delirium, fever and despair. But he has to be the one who gives the orders and he always refuses to pay attention to us when we need him.

After the time when I lived in the south I got to know grief very well—a real, irremediable and incurable grief that shattered my life, and when I tried to put it together again I realized that I and my life had become something irreconcilable with what had gone before. Only my vocation remained unchanged, but it is profoundly misleading to say that even that was unchanged— the tools were still the same but the way I used them had altered. At first I hated it, it disgusted me, but I knew very well that I would end up returning to it, and that it would save me. Sometimes I would think that I had not been so unfortunate in my life and that I was unjust when I accused destiny of never having shown me any kindness, because it had given me my three children and my vocation. Besides, I could not imagine my life without my vocation. It was always there, it had never left me for a moment, and when I believed that it slept its vigilant, shining eyes were still watching me.

Such is my vocation. It does not produce much money and it is always necessary to follow some other vocation simultaneously in order to live. Though sometimes it produces a little, and it is very satisfying to have money because of it—it is like receiving money and presents from the hands of someone you love. Such is my vocation. I do not, I repeat, know much about the value of the results it has given me or could give me; or it would be better to say that I know the relative though certainly not the absolute value of the results I have already obtained. When I write something I usually think it is very important and that I am a very fine writer. I think this happens to everyone. But there is one corner of my mind in which I know very well what I am, which is a small, a very small writer. I swear I know it. But that doesn't matter much to me. Only I don't want to think about names: I can see that if I am asked "A small writer like who?" it would sadden me to think of the names of other small writers. I prefer to think that no one has ever been like me, however small, however much a mosquito or a flea of a writer I may be. The important thing is to be convinced that this really is your vocation, your profession, something you will do all your life. But as a vocation it is no joke. There are innumerable dangers besides those I have mentioned. We are constantly threatened with grave dangers whenever we write a page. There is the danger of suddenly starting to be flirtatious and of singing. I always have a crazy desire to sing and I have to be very careful that I don't. And there is the danger of cheating with words that do not really exist within us, that we have picked up by chance from outside of ourselves and which we skillfully slip in because we have become a bit dishonest. There is the danger of cheating and being dishonest. As you see, it is quite a difficult vocation, but it is the finest one in the world. The days and houses of our lives, the days and houses of the people with whom we are involved, books and images and thoughts and conversations—all these things feed it, and it grows within us. It is a vocation which also feeds on terrible things; it swallows the best and the worst in our lives and our evil feelings flow in its blood just as much as our benevolent feelings. It feeds itself and grows within us.

URSULA K. LE GUIN

THE WRITER ON, AND AT, HER WORK

Her work
is never done.
She has been told that
and observed it for herself.
    Her work
spins unrelated filaments
into a skein: the whorl
or wheel turns the cloudy mass
into one strong thread,
over, and over, and over.
    Her work
weaves unrelated elements
into a pattern: the shuttle
thrown across the warp
makes roses, mazes, lightning,
over, and over, and over.
    Her work
brings out of dirt and water
a whole thing, a hole where
the use of the pot is,
a container for the thing
contained, a holy thing, a holder,
a saver,
happening on the clayey wheel
between her and her clayey hands,
over, and over, and over.
    Her work
is with pots and baskets,
bags, cans, boxes, carryalls,
pans, jars, pitchers, cupboards, closets,
rooms, rooms in houses, doors,

desks in the rooms in the houses,
drawers and pigeonholes in the desks,
secret compartments
in which lie for generations
secret letters.
            Her work
is with letters,
with secret letters.
Letters that were not written
for generations.
She must write them
over, and over, and over.

She works with her body,
a day-laborer.
She labors, she travails,
sweating and complaining.
She is her instrument,
whorl, shuttle, wheel.
She is the greasy wool and the raw clay
and the wise hands
that work by day
for the wages of the worker.

She works within her body,
a night creature.
She runs between the walls.
She is hunted down and eaten.
She prowls, pounces, kills, devours.
She flies on soundless wings.
Her eyes comprehend the darkness.
The tracks she leaves are bloody,
and at her scream
everything holds still,
hearing that other wisdom.

        Some say any woman working
is a warrior.
I resist that definition.
A fighter in necessity, sure,
a wise fighter,

but a professional?
One of los Generales?
Seems to me she has better things
to do than be a hero.
Medals were made for flatter chests.
They sort of dangle off her tits
and look embarrassing.
The uniforms don't fit.
If she shoots from the hip,
she hears the freudians applauding—
See? See? they say,
See? See? She wants one!
(She wants mine!
She can't have it!
She can't can she Daddy?
                    No, son.)

        Others say she's a goddess,
The Goddess, transcendent,
knowing everything by nature,
the Archetype
at the typewriter.
I resist that definition.

Her work, I really think her work
isn't fighting, isn't winning,
isn't being the Earth, isn't being the Moon.
Her work, I really think her work
is finding what her real work is
and doing it,
her work, her own work,
her being human,
her being in the world.

        So, if I am
a writer, my work
is words. Unwritten letters.

Words are my way of being
human, woman, me.
Word is the whorl that spins me,

-the shuttle thrown through the warp of years
to weave a life, the hand
that shapes to use, to grace.
Word is my tooth,
my wing.
Word is my wisdom.

I am a bundle of letters
in a secret drawer
in an old desk.
What is in the letters?
What do they say?

I am kept here a prisoner by the evil Duke.

Georgie is much better now, and I have been canning peaches like mad.

I cannot tell my husband or even my sister, I cannot live without you, I think of you day and night, when will you come to me?

My brother Will hath gone to London and though I begg'd with all my heart to go with him nor he nor my Father would have it so, but laugh'd and said, Time the wench was married.

The ghost of a woman walks in this house. I have heard her weeping in the room that was used as a nursery.

If I only knew that my letters were reaching you, but there is no way to get information at any of the bureaus, they will not say where you have been sent.

Don't grieve for me. I know what I am doing.

Bring the kids and they can all play together and we can sit and talk till we're blue in the face.

Did he know about her cousin Roger and the shotgun?

I don't know if it's any good but I've been working on it ever since September.

How many of us will it take to hang him?

I am taking the family to America, the land of Freedom.

I have found a bundle of old letters in a secret compartment in my desk.

> Letters of words of stories:
> they tell stories.
> The writer tells stories, the stories,
> over, and over, and over.
>
> Man does, they say, and Woman is.
> Doing and being. Do and be.
> O.K., I be writing, Man.
> I be telling. ("Je suis là où ça parle,"
> says la belle Hélène.)
> I be saying and parlaying.
> I be being
> this way. How do I do being?
> Same way I be doing.
> I would call it working,
> or else, it doesn't matter, playing.
> The writer at her work
> is playing.
> Not chess not poker not monopoly,
> none of the war games—
> Even if she plays by all their rules,
> and wins—wins what?
> Their funny money?—
> not playing hero,
> not playing god—
> well, but listen, making things
> is a kind of godly business, isn't it?—
> All right, then, playing god:
> Aphrodite the Maker, without whom
> "nothing is born into the shining
> borders of light, nor is anything lovely or lovable made,"
> Spider Grandmother, spinning,
> Thought Woman, making it all up,

Coyote Woman, playing—
playing it, a game,
without a winner or a loser,
a game of skill, a game of make
believe.

Sure it's a gamble,
but not for money.
Sorry Ernie this ain't stud.
The stakes
are a little higher.

     The writer at her work
is odd, is peculiar, is particular,
certainly, but not, I think,
singular.
She tends to the plural.

I for example am Ursula; Miss
Ursula Kroeber;
Mrs. then Ms. Le Guin;
Ursula K. Le Guin; this latter is
"the writer," but who were,
who are, the others?
She is the writer
at their work.

     What are they doing,
those plurals of her?
Lying in bed.
Lazy as hound dogs.
She-Plural is lying in bed
in the morning early.
Long before light, in winter;
in summer "the morning people
are chirping on the roof."
And like the sparrows
her thoughts go hopping
and flying and trying out words.
And like the light of morning

her thought impalpably touches
shape, and reveals it,
brings seeing from dimness,
being from inexhaustible chaos.

That is the good time.
That is the time when this she-plural writer
finds what is to be written.
In the first light,
seeing with the eyes
of the child waking,
lying between sleep and the day
in the body of dream,
in the body of flesh
that has been/is
a fetus, a baby, a child, a girl, a woman, a lover, a mother,
has contained other bodies,
incipient beings, minds unawakened, not to awaken,
has been sick, been damaged, been healed,
been old, is born and dying, will die,
in the mortal, inexhaustible
body
of her work:

That is the good time.

Spinning the fleece of the sun, that cloudy mass,
weaving a glance and a gesture,
shaping the clay of emotion;
housekeeping. Patterning.
Following patterns.
Lying there
in the dreamtime
following patterns.

        So then you have to cut it out—
take a deep breath,
the first cut, the blank page!—
and sew it together (drudgery,
toil in the sacred sweatshop)—
the garment, the soul-coat,
the thing made of words,

cloth of the sunfleece,
the new clothes of the Emperor.

(Yes, and some kid comes along
and yaps, "But he hasn't any clothes on!"
Muzzle the brat
till it learns
that none of us has any clothes on,
that our souls are naked,
dressed in words only,
in charity only,
the gift of the others.
Any fool can see through it.
Only fools say so.)

      Long ago when I was Ursula
writing, but not "the writer,"
and not very plural yet,
and worked with the owls not the sparrows,
being young, scribbling at midnight:

I came to a place
I couldn't see well in the darkness,
where the road turned
and divided, it seemed like,
going different ways.
I was lost.
I didn't know which way.
It looked like one roadsign said To Town
and the other didn't say anything.

So I took the way that didn't say.
I followed
myself.
"I don't care," I said,
terrified.
"I don't care if nobody ever reads it!
I'm going *this* way."

And I found myself
in the dark forest, in silence.

You maybe have to find yourself,
your selves,
in the dark forest.
Anyhow, I did then. And still now,
always. At the bad time.

        When you find the hidden catch
in the secret drawer
behind the false panel
inside the concealed compartment
in the desk in the attic
of the house in the dark forest,
and press the spring firmly,
a door flies open to reveal
a bundle of old letters,
and in one of them
is a map
of the forest
that you drew yourself
before you ever went there.

        The Writer at her Work:
I see her walking
on a path through a pathless forest,
or a maze, a labyrinth.
As she walks she spins,
and the fine thread falls behind her
following her way,
telling
where she is going,
where she has gone.
Telling the story.
The line, the thread of voice,
the sentences saying the way.

        The Writer on her Work:
I see her, too, I see her
lying on it.
Lying, in the morning early,
rather uncomfortable.
Trying to convince herself

that it's a bed of roses,
a bed of laurels,
or an innerspring mattress,
or anyhow a futon.
But she keeps twitching.

There's a *lump*, she says.
There's something
like a *rock*—like a *lentil*—
I can't sleep.

There's *something*
the size of a split pea
that I haven't written.
That I haven't written right.
I can't sleep.

She gets up
and writes it.
Her work
is never done.

NOTES ON CONTRIBUTORS

MARGARET ATWOOD was born in Ottawa, Ontario, in 1939 and was educated at the University of Toronto, Radcliffe College, and Harvard University. Her first novel *The Edible Woman* was published in 1969, followed by *Surfacing, Lady Oracle, Life Before Man, Bodily Harm* and *The Handmaid's Tale*, winner of both the Arthur C. Clarke Award for Science Fiction and the Governor-General's Award. It was also shortlisted for the Booker Prize—and is now a major film. She has also published three collections of short stories, *Dancing Girls, Bluebeard's Egg* and *Wilderness Tips*, as well as fifteen volumes of poetry. Her most recent novel, *Cat's Eye*, published in 1989, was also shortlisted for the Booker Prize. Margaret Atwood lives in Toronto with the writer Graeme Gibson and their daughter.

TONI CADE BAMBARA was born and brought up in Harlem, New York, the setting of many of her stories. A former Rutgers University professor, she now lives with her daughter Karma in Atlanta, Georgia, and lectures in the North-East and on the West Coast of America. Her publications include *Gorilla My Love* (1972), *Sea Birds Are Still Alive* and *The Salt Eaters*.

ANITA DESAI's most recent novel is *Baumgartner's Bombay*, published by Knopf in 1989. Born of Bengali and German parents in 1937 in Mussoorie, India, she was educated in Delhi. Her novel *Clear Light of Day* was nominated for the Booker Prize (1980), as was *In Custody* (1984). *Fire on the Mountain* received both the Royal Society of Literature's Winifred Holtby Memorial Prize and the 1978 National Academy of Letters Award (Delhi). She has also written children's books and a book of short stories, *Games at Twilight*. A fellow of the Royal Society of Literature in London, she is also a Fellow of Girton College, Cambridge, and has taught writing at Smith College and Mount Holyoke College in the United States. Married with four children, she currently resides in South Hadley, Massachusetts.

JOAN DIDION was born in Sacramento, California, and graduated from the University of California at Berkeley. On winning first prize in the Vogue magazine Prix de Paris writing competition, she travelled east, worked at

Vogue, and wrote her first novel, *Run River* (1963). She returned to California and has published three other novels, *Play It As It Lays, A Book of Common Prayer*, and *Democracy*, as well as two collections of essays, *Slouching Towards Bethlehem* and *The White Album*, and two books of reportage, *Salvador* and, most recently, *Miami* (1987). She has co-written a number of screenplays with her husband, among them dramatizations of *Play It As It Lays, The Panic in Needle Park*, and *A Star Is Born*, and contributes regularly to various magazines including *The New York Review of Books* and *The New Yorker*.

NATALIA GINZBURG's body of work in English translation includes the autobiographical novel *Family Sayings* (1984) and the novels *All Our Yesterdays* and *The City and the House*. A playwright and critic, she has also written a collection of essays, *The Little Virtues*, and the nonfiction work *Serena Cruz, or True Justice*, recently pubished in Italy. Born in Palermo in 1916, she grew up in Turin, where she worked as a publisher and writer. In 1938 she married Leone Ginzburg, and was active with him in anti-Fascist causes; they and their three children were confined by the Fascists in the Abruzzi region in the 1940s. In 1943 they went to Rome, where her husband was arrested by the Germans; he died in prison in 1944. After the war she became an editor at the publishing house Einaudi. She has translated Proust and Flaubert into Italian; she was also elected a senator in the Italian Parliament in 1983 and played a small role in Pasolini's *The Gospel According to Saint Matthew*. Her two sons are university professors and her daughter is a psychoanalyst. Since 1950, Ginzburg has lived in Rome.

MARY GORDON was born in Far Rockaway, New York. She attended Barnard College and the Writing Program at Syracuse University. Her first novel, *Final Payments*, was nominated for the National Book Critics Circle award in 1978. She has since published three novels, *The Company of Women, Men and Angels* and *The Other Side* (1990), as well as a collection of stories, *Temporary Shelter* and a collection of essays, *Good Boys and Dead Girls*. Her short stories have been published in *Ms., The Ladies' Home Journal, Mademoiselle, Virginia Quarterly Review*, and *Southern Review*. She lives in upstate New York with her husband and two children.

DIANE JOHNSON was born in 1934 in Moline, Illinois. She was educated at Stephens College and the University of Utah, and received her M.A. and Ph.D. from UCLA. Her novels include *Fair Game* (1965), *The Shadow*

Knows, and *Lying Low*, which was nominated for the National Book Award for Fiction in 1979. She has received a Guggenheim Fellowship (1977–78), as well as the Rosenthal Award and The Strauss Living from the American Academy of Arts and Letters (1979). Her nonfiction work includes *Lesser Lives: The Biography of the First Mrs. Meredith*, the essay collection *Terrorists and Novelists*, and *Dashiell Hammett: A Life*. She has adapted *The Shadow Knows* as a screenplay and also the Stephen King novel, *The Shining*, in collaboration with writer/director Stanley Kubrick. A frequent contributor to *The New York Review of Books*, she has been professor of English at the University of California at Davis. Her new novel, *Health and Happiness*, was published by Knopf in 1990. The mother of four grown children, she now divides her time between San Francisco and Paris, and is writing "a sort of travel book in which the heroine of *Persian Nights* sees something more of the world."

ELIZABETH JOLLEY was born in 1923 near Birmingham, England, of Austrian-British parentage. Educated in a Quaker boarding school, she served as a nurse in the Second World War. In 1959 she emigrated to Western Australia, where she now lives with her husband, Leonard. She teaches at the Curtin University of Technology, conducts writing workshops in remote country areas and in prisons, and raises geese and fruit trees on a small rural farm. Her first book, *The Five Acre Virgin and Other Stories*, appeared in 1976; since then she has published twelve books, among them the novels *Foxybaby*, *The Sugar Mother* and, most recently, *My Father's Moon* (1989) and *Cabin Fever* (1990), as well as a number of plays for radio. Her works have been translated into German, French, Spanish, and Russian; among her many honors, she was the 1988 recipient of the Canada/Australia Literary Prize. The title for her essay in this collection is a quote from Alexander Pope.

ERICA JONG is the author of six books of poetry, *Fruits & Vegetables* (1971), *Half-lives, Loveroot, At the Edge of the Body, Ordinary Miracles* and *Becoming Light* (1991). She has also written six novels, *Fear of Flying* (1973), *How To Save Your Own Life, Fanny, Being the True History of Fanny Hackabout Jones, Parachutes & Kisses, Serenissima* and *Any Woman's Blues*. She has also written a children's book, *Megan's Book of Divorce*, and the nonfiction book *Witches*. A native New Yorker, she now divides her time between New York City and Connecticut, with her daughter, Molly.

MAXINE HONG KINGSTON was born in Stockton, California, in 1940. Her first book *The Woman Warrior: Memoirs of a Girlhood among Ghosts*, won the National Book Critics Circle award as the best book of nonfiction published in 1976. Her stories and essays have appeared in *The New York Times, Ms., The New Yorker, American Heritage*, and *New West*. She has published a second book of nonfiction, *China Men*, and her first novel, *Tripmaster Monkey – His Fake Book* in 1989. She has held National Endowment for the Arts and Guggenheim Fellowships.

URSULA K. LE GUIN was born in 1929 in Berkeley, California, daughter of writer Theodora Kroeber and anthropologist Alfred L. Kroeber. Educated at Radcliffe College and Columbia University, she has received several Hugo and Nebula awards for her speculative fiction, including *The Left Hand of Darkness* (1969) and *The Dispossessed* (1974), *The Farthest Shore* (1972) won a National Book Award. In addition to her fifteen novels, she has published four volumes of short stories, as well as a screenplay, *King Dog*, children's books, poetry and collections of critical essays. Her most recent collection of stories is *Buffalo Gals* (1987). Married to historian Charles A. Le Guin in 1953, she is the mother of three grown children; she presently lives in Oregon.

JAN MORRIS was born in 1926 of Anglo-Welsh parents. She was educated at Oxford and spent a year on a Commonwealth Fellowship in the United States. She worked for ten years as a foreign correspondent, covering sundry wars, coups and rebellions, besides reporting the first ascent of Mount Everest in 1953 and making the first motor-crossing of Oman in 1956. She has published more than 20 books, including the Pax Britannica trilogy about the British Empire, works on Wales, Venice, Spain, New York, Hong Kong and Oxford, and six volumes of collected travel essays. Her novel *Last Letter From Hav* was a finalist for the Booker Prize in 1985, and she was the editor of *The Oxford Book of Oxford*. Ms. Morris wrote as James Morris until the change of sexual identity which was chronicled in her 1974 book *Conundrum*. Jan Morris lives in Wales.

BHARATI MUKHERJEE was born in Calcutta and lived in Canada with her husband, writer Clark Blaise, before emigrating to the United States. She attended college in India and also the University of Iowa, where she received an M.F.A. and Ph.D. She won the National Book of Critics Circle Award in fiction for *The Middleman and Other Stories*, becoming the first naturalized American citizen to do so. Her other writings include *Darkness* (1985), a collection of stories; *Days and Nights in Calcutta*, a travel memoir co-authored with her husband; and a novel, *Jasmine* (1989). At Emory University in Atlanta she was writer-in-residence in 1984; she has also taught creative writing at Columbia University, New York University, and Queens College, and is now a professor in the English Department of the University of California at Berkeley. She and her husband have two grown sons.

JANET STERNBURG was born in Boston, Massachusetts, and received a degree in philosophy from the New School for Social Research in New York. A poet and essayist, as well as writer for theater and film, she has a special interest in women and creativity. For film, she has produced and directed the award-winning public television portrait *Virginia Woolf: The Moment Whole* (1971); for theater, she has adapted and staged the works of Colette, Louise Bogan, H.D., and Isak Dinesen for the Manhattan Theater Club, where she served as director of the Writers in Performance series. Her work on and about other artists also includes the films *El Teatro Campesino* and *Thomas Eakins: A Motion Portrait*, as well as the series *Likely Stories* (1987). Her poems and essays have been widely published in anthologies and journals, and she has received a scriptwriting award from the National Endowment for the Humanities. Married to college president Steven Lavine, she divides her time between New York, where she serves as media consultant to the Rockefeller Foundation, and Los Angeles, where she teaches creative writing at the California Institute of the Arts. She is currently curating a television series of films by women and working on a collection of her personal essays.

ANNE TYLER is the author of ten novels, among them *Earthly Possessions* (1977), *Searching for Caleb, Morgan's Passing, Dinner at the Homesick Restaurant, The Accidental Tourist* (1985, made into a major film in 1989), and most recently, *Saint Maybe* (1991). She was born in Minneapolis, Minnesota, in 1941, but grew up in Raleigh, North Carolina, and considers herself a southerner. She was graduated at nineteen from Duke University, where she twice won the Anne Flexner Award for creative writing. She has done graduate work in Russian studies at Columbia University and worked for a year as the Russian bibliographer at the Duke University Library. Her stories have appeared in many magazines, among them *The New Yorker* and *Harper's*. The mother of two children, she is married to a psychiatrist, Taghi Mohammad Modaressi, and makes her home in Baltimore, Maryland.

ALICE WALKER was born in Georgia in 1944, attended Spelman College, and graduated from Sarah Lawrence College. She is the author of five books of poems. *Once, Revolutionary Petunias, Good Night Willie Lee, I'll See You in the Morning* and *Horses Make a Landscape Look More Beautiful*. She has published four novels, *The Third Life of Grange Copeland* (1970), *Meridian, The Color Purple* (1982, which won the Pulitzer Prize and the American Book Award and was made into a feature film); her most recent is *The Temple of My Familiar*, (1989). Two collections of her stories have been published, *In Love & Trouble* and *Stories of Black*, as well as a collection of essays, *In Search of Our Mothers' Gardens: Womanish Prose*. For many years she has taught courses in writing, black literature, and women writers. She has been a scholar at the Bread Loaf Writers' Conference and a fellow at the Radcliffe Institute. She has lived in Jackson, Mississippi, where she was actively involved in voter registration, and now lives in California with her daughter.

MARGARET WALKER was born in Birmingham, Alabama, in 1915. She graduated from Northwestern University and received her Master of Arts from the University of Iowa, where her thesis was a book of poetry, *For My People*, which in 1942 won the Yale Award for Younger Poets. Her Civil War novel, *Jubilee*, has been translated into seven languages; her other books are *Prophets for a New Day, October Journey, A Poetic Equation: Conversations between Nikki Giovanni and Margaret Walker, Richard Wright: Daemonic Genius, This is My Century* and, most recently, *How I Wrote Jubilee and Other Essays on Literature and Life*, edited by Maryemma Graham, 1990. Among her many honors are a Houghton Mifflin Literary Fellowship and a senior fellowship from the National Endowment for the Humanities. At Jackson State University, from which she has now retired, she was professor of English and director of the Institute for the Study of History, Life and Culture of Black People.

Other Virago Books of Interest

A LITERATURE OF THEIR OWN:
From Charlotte Brontë to Doris Lessing
Elaine Showalter

'Elaine Showalter's proceedings in this book, both as historian and as literary critic, are sane, illuminating, fascinating and wise' – *A. S. Byatt, The Times*

'An important, even classic book. It must serve as an essential starting point for every serious student of women's writing' – *Margaret Walters*

In this brilliant study of British women novelists, Elaine Showalter traces the development of their fiction from the 1800s onwards. This original, refreshing and sometimes controversial book not only includes assessments of famous writers such as the Brontës, George Eliot, Virginia Woolf, Margaret Drabble and Doris Lessing, but also presents critical appraisals of Mary Braddon, Rhoda Broughton and Sarah Grand – to name but a few of those prolific and successful Victorian novelists – once household names, now largely forgotten.

The result is an invaluable record of generations of women writers and the way in which their work reflects the social changes of their time.

A VERY GREAT PROFESSION:
The Woman's Novel 1914–39

Nicola Beauman

'Katharine, thus, was a member of a very great profession which has, as yet, no title and very little recognition . . . She lived at home' – *Virginia Woolf, Night and Day*

In this book, Nicola Beauman looks at women like Katharine, or like Laura, the heroine of *Brief Encounter*, women whose lives and habits are wonderfully recorded in the fiction of the time. Drawing on the novels to illuminate themes as varied as domestic life, romantic love, sex, psychoanalysis, war and 'surplus' women, Nicola Beauman uses the work of such diverse women novelists as May Sinclair and Elinor Glyn, Rebecca West and E. M. Delafield, Rosamond Lehmann and Mary Borden – and many, many more – to present a fascinating portrait, through their fiction, of middle-class Englishwomen in the period between the wars.

'A very broad, good guide to a lot of forgotten things . . . people are going to enjoy reading it' – *Margaret Drabble*

'Infinitely sharp, subtle and entertaining' – *Molly Keane*

'Miss Beauman's survey is sympathetic, even affectionate, her analysis very thorough – *Penelope Mortimer*

'Nicola Beauman has read and read, with passionate enthusiasm and infectious enjoyment' – *Susan Hill*

WOMEN WRITING ABOUT MEN
Jane Miller

'*Women Writing About Men* is one of the most intelligent works of feminist literary criticisms that I have read' – *Literary Review*

'An absorbing and extremely intelligent addition, from an original angle, to the canon of feminist critiques of women's writing . . . shows women "transforming themselves from men's heroines to the tellers of their own stories"' – *Hermione Lee*

This fascinating book is about novels by women and about the men in them. It is also about women reading, and the sense we make of other women's accounts of the world. Its focus is the novel as a form which women writers, from the early nineteenth century to the present day, have used to question and challenge men's appropriation of women's experience, and to explore their own perspectives on men as husbands, fathers, brothers, sons and lovers. Drawing on the work of writers from Jane Austen, the Brontës and George Eliot, to Dorothy Richardson, Rebecca West, Virginia Woolf, Doris Lessing, Christina Stead, Angela Carter, Alice Walker and many more, Jane Miller's exciting and original study offers important new perspectives on women and men and on writing.

INVENTED LIVES:
Narratives of Black Women 1860–1960
Mary Helen Washington

'Ms Washington has created a most engaging dialogue between the great black women writers and herself. This collection is, in fact, two fine books in one: at once an anthology and a critical study' – *New York Times*

In this marvellous companion volume to her anthology of stories by black women writers, *Any Woman's Blues*, Mary Helen Washington explores the works, and the worlds, of black American women writers between 1860 and 1960. Bringing together selected short stories and novel extracts from ten writers – Harriet Jacobs, Frances Ellen Watkins Harper, Pauline E. Hopkins, Fannie Barrier Williams, Marita Bonner, Nella Larsen, Zora Neale Hurston, Ann Petry, Dorothy West and Gwendolyn Brooks – she introduces a remarkable range of voices and draws out the hidden and overt challenges of a body of work rich in cultural, political and literary meaning. *Invented Lives* also includes an Introduction and six chapters in which Mary Helen Washington examines black women writers' search for a narrative structure appropriate to their experiences in American society. The result is a stunning collection of prose and an eloquent affirmation of a neglected literary tradition.

VIRTUE OF NECESSITY:
English Women's Writing 1649–88
Elaine Hobby

'This courageous book is full of information and new ideas ... It opens up whole new areas ... splendid' – *Christopher Hill*

In this fascinating survey of some two hundred women's writings between 1640–88, Elaine Hobby draws on the extraordinary range of genres in which women expressed themselves in petitions, prophecies and religious writings, autobiography and biography, fiction, plays, poetry, and books on housewifery, medicine, midwifery and education. Living under the 'necessity' of their subjection, their writings show us how they were able to make a virtue of this – to turn constraints into permissions, into little pockets of liberty or autonomy, thus constantly defining and redefining existing concepts of femininity. In the upheavals of civil war and regicide, many women travelled the country and even the world, campaigning for social change and explaining their beliefs. In 1649, for example, Joanna Cartwright appealed for Jews to be readmitted to England and many petitions sought parliamentary reforms for women.

After the restoration of the monarchy in 1660, women such as these were driven back into quiescence. Others turned to love poetry and plays, often ridiculing male conventions of panting lovers and coy mistresses: Aphra Behn, reviled for her success as a woman playwright, nevertheless wove together with wit and humour, music and spectacle, the dilemmas that she and her sisters faced in the debauchery of the Restoration. *Virtue of Necessity* makes a major contribution to our understanding of women's literary activity and lives in the seventeenth century.

THE SIGN OF ANGELLICA:
Women, Writing and Fiction 1660–1800
Janet Todd

'A model of clarity and careful construction . . . hugely informative . . . an indispensible book' – *Helen Wilcox, Times Higher Education Supplement*

In this scholarly and entertaining work, Janet Todd takes as her subject the entry of women into literature as a profession in the Restoration and eighteenth century. She richly explores the various signs that women deployed during this crucial period for the construction of the modern ideology of femininity. Angellica in Aphra Behn's *The Rover* deliberately hangs out a seductive sign of womanhood the better to sell herself. Over a hundred years later Mary Wollstonecraft also asserted that femininity was a cultural construction and that writing was an act of self-assertion for women. But between Behn and Wollstonecraft lies a century of changing strategies of authorship employed by women: the erotic and witty invitations to men in the Restoration; the sentimental appeal to modesty, passivity, chastity in the mid-century in which the authors kept their signs indoors, writing simply as 'a lady' or 'one of the fair sex'; the assumption of moral authority at the century's close.

Janet Todd studies private letters as well as public dramas, but it is fiction in particular that is seen as self-expression; as an investigation of women's social and psychological predicament, and as a communal female dream. Extended essays on authors such as the Duchess of Newcastle, Eliza Haywood, Charlotte Lennox, Sarah Fielding, Ann Radcliffe, and Fanny Burney elaborate her engaging and persuasive thesis.